# STUDIES IN THE LANGUAGE OF ST. PAUL

# STUDIES IN THE LANGUAGE OF ST. PAUL

BY

R. MARTIN POPE, M.A., B.D.

*Honorary Lecturer in Hellenistic Greek and
Early Christian Literature,
University College,
Southampton*

WIPF & STOCK · Eugene, Oregon

Wipf and Stock Publishers
199 W 8th Ave, Suite 3
Eugene, OR 97401

Studies in the Language of St. Paul
By Pope, R. Martin
Softcover ISBN-13: 978-1-7252-7399-3
Publication date 3/18/2020
Previously published by Epworth, 1936

# CONTENTS

| CHAP. | | PAGE |
|---|---|---|
| | PREFACE | 7 |
| I. | THE PEACE OF GOD | 11 |
| II. | THE TRIUMPH-JOY | 19 |
| III. | A GOOD DEGREE | 27 |
| IV. | FORBEARANCE | 33 |
| V. | REDEEMING THE TIME | 41 |
| VI. | BOLDNESS OF SPEECH | 48 |
| VII. | EARNEST EXPECTATION | 55 |
| VIII. | SINCERITY | 63 |
| IX. | A GOOD REPORT FROM WITHOUT | 72 |
| X. | THE UNATTAINED IDEAL | 78 |
| XI. | BONDS AND THE UNBOUND WORD | 85 |
| XII. | ENDURANCE | 94 |
| XIII. | THE PERPETUAL OPPORTUNITY | 102 |
| XIV. | THE HEAVENLY PLACES | 110 |
| XV. | CONTENTMENT | 118 |
| XVI. | THE MIRROR AND THE RIDDLE | 125 |
| XVII. | INDWELLING POWER | 135 |
| XVIII. | THE THIRD HEAVEN | 141 |
| XIX. | HYPERBOLES OF FAITH | 149 |
| | GREEK WORDS | 157 |

# PREFACE

THE following expositions are an attempt to elucidate the teaching of St. Paul by means of a careful scrutiny of his vocabulary. They are in effect studies of his words and phrases. He composed his letters in a style of marked individuality, using the language of his day as a medium for conveying to his fellow-Christians his personal experience of the new faith, with an emotional intensity and with a depth of conviction peculiarly his own. Let no one imagine that his Greek is not literary because he wrote in the idiom of the popular or 'common' tongue current from 300 B.C. in the lands bordering the Mediterranean. Christianity created new terms and at the same time imparted to old and familiar words a freshness born of an original vision of truth. It is with reluctance that I have decided to transliterate the original words instead of printing them in their own noble type, but I have had in view the needs of students who have no knowledge of Greek. Yet I am not without the hope that these studies may assist readers of New Testament Greek, whose duty it is to ascertain the etymology, meaning and usage of the terms used in the text. Occasionally the terms are peculiar to St. Paul, though not for that reason always to be considered his coinages and are often susceptible to various interpretations. Lexical study, especially in the light of recent papyri discoveries, is a fascinating side of the student's task, although its value is not always realized, and for the convenience of those who engage in it, I have given in an appendix a list of the Greek words discussed in these pages.

Some of the studies appeared originally in a volume entitled the *Poetry of the Upward Way*, and were republished in a cheap form under a title which I am repeating, *Studies in the Language of St. Paul*. This latter edition was speedily exhausted and the demand induced me to undertake a further series of studies on the same lines, which, owing to the encouragement of the late Dr. James Hastings, found a home in the *Expository Times* and which have never been republished in book form. Thus the present volume is, to a considerable extent, a new collection with the addition of the older studies revised and rearranged.

Having been in contact for many years with young people and adults, who have been induced to learn Greek in order the better to understand the New Testament, I can bear witness to the new and vivid interest which even an elementary acquaintance with the language can impart to the study of these great writings. Hence my hope is that the following experiments may be a guide to students and preachers, and further may stimulate in not a few a desire to master a language which a recent writer, Dr. B. F. C. Atkinson, in his *Study of the Greek Language*

(p. 291), has described as 'the language of humanity . . . because it speaks to and satisfies the deepest needs of humanity'; while the New Testament is 'the monument that carries the Greek language and the Greek mode of expression into the heart of the world and its power was never so apparent as it is to-day.'

It is hardly necessary to add that only a corner of a large field is here explored, but what has been attempted may inspire others to engage in the work and incidentally may serve to show that the preacher, who must ever be an expositor, can find in his textbook a treasure from which he can bring forth 'things new and old.'

I have endeavoured to record in the text or footnotes my obligations to interpreters of St. Paul and other writers who have thrown light on the subjects discussed. In particular, my thanks are due to Messrs. Macmillan & Co., the publishers of F. W. H. Myers' *St. Paul,* for permission to quote freely from that poem in two of the chapters, and to Messrs. George Allen & Unwin, Ltd., the publishers of the translation of the *Bacchae* of Euripides by Professor Gilbert Murray, for permission to quote the three extracts on p. 21.

R. Martin Pope.

# STUDIES IN THE LANGUAGE OF ST. PAUL

## CHAPTER I

## THE PEACE OF GOD

St. Paul never begins an epistle without a salutation containing the word 'peace' (*eirēnē*). And in the body of his teaching 'peace' plays a conspicuous part. God is a 'God of *peace*.' The Christian has '*peace* with God.' 'To be spiritually minded is life and *peace*.' It is obvious that he lays much stress on the possession of this golden treasure of inward peace. With him it implies the removal of the guilt that separated us from God, the assurance of pardon, and the conformity of our will with His. He never uses the word to imply that peace in the sense of being in harmony with our surroundings is attainable here. Indeed, he startles us by bringing the word 'peace' into associations with which at first sight it appears to be incongruous. There are two passages which are especially worthy of our attention by reason of the beauty and unexpectedness of the metaphors used by the Apostle. In one of them he speaks of peace as an *arbitrator ;* in the other of peace as a *sentinel*. The atmosphere is that of a conflict, yet peace lives on in the strife. It can, therefore, be no earthly product. It cometh from above. It lies exposed to all the shocks and invasions of earthly things. It is not exempt from the blows of sorrow, hardship, persecution, and death. But it survives all these things. It is—to use Wordsworth's well-known words—

> A central peace subsisting at the heart
> Of endless agitation.

1. Peace is an *arbitrator* (*brabeus*) : 'Let the peace of God rule (*brabeuetō*) in your hearts' (Col. iii. 15). But the colourless word 'rule' becomes 'arbitrate' in the margin of the Revisers. The expression suggests an umpire who decides in a contest and awards the prize to a victor. There were ten judges in the Greek Olympian games, where the winners received a wreath of the sacred wild olive. But, according to Alexander Maclaren, we may give a more familiar shape to the figure if we turn to medieval days and conceive of peace as the queen of the tournament, whose eyes 'rain influence, and judge the prize.' Thus the soul of the Christian is an arena. Two forces—flesh and spirit—contend daily for supremacy. Desire and conscience, passion and duty, the knowledge of the right and 'the vainglory of life'—these are in constant conflict within us. The best and the worst, motives noble and ignoble, fight for possession, for mastery. The pain of bearing a cross and a burden, which means the deepening of love and patience and purity, strives

against the joy of self-indulgence, which issues in callousness, incompetence, and hatred. Now, the peace of God sits on the throne of our hearts to decide between the combatants, to close the strife, and to deck with the victor's crown triumphant fortitude.

Let it be noted, it is not the peace of man; for the peace of man, as Chrysostom reminds us, is begotten of self-preservation, of shrinking back, of suffering nothing grievous. The peace of man inevitably favours the lower elements of character. It stops the inward strife by the concession of the flesh. It urges us to throw away our shield and to trample on conviction. It is a cowardly spirit, abhorring the pains of sacrifice and the taking up of the cross. The peace of God awards the prize only to the noblest self. It urges to heroic self-conquest, and rewards the victory of light, truth, sincerity, and the forces that make for righteousness. When sin gains possession, then we know that the peace of God has been dethroned. The storm has begun which is to wreck the fair beauty and happiness of the soul. It dashes the flowers to the ground, and strips the forest of its green leaves. 'The overflowing scourge' passes through, and 'the crown of pride is trodden under foot.' How swiftly the shadow of the coming unrest falls when the careless word has been spoken, bringing pain to a sensitive spirit, or when the hasty temper has left its wounds, or when the selfish deed has darkened the sunshine of others. Then we know that the peace of God has not been arbitrator. The joy of self-conquest has been forfeited. No laurel crown has been granted to the daring and to the beauty of holiness.

There is a line in a well-known hymn which conveys, through quite different associations, the same lesson as St. Paul's figure. The hymn is an invocation to the Holy Spirit, and speaks of His work as

> Thy halcyon rest within,
> Calming the storms of dread and sin.

Halcyon—so goes the legend—in despair at finding the body of her drowned husband on the shore, throws herself into the sea and is changed with him into a kingfisher. And the story further shows that for seven days before and after the shortest day, while the kingfishers build their nests, the sea is calm. Hence Milton, in his ode on the Nativity, speaks of the 'birds of calm' that 'sit brooding on the charmèd wave.' Thus is the 'halcyon rest' none other than the peace of God. For on the wintry days of the soul, days of storm and stress, of snow and sadness, the mystic bird of calm is to spread his wings over us and to charm the waves into stillness. Let us enthrone the peace of God within as the arbiter of our hearts. Then shall our false ambitions and desires be subdued. Then shall our base passions, our harsh moods, our high aspiring thoughts, be brought into the obedience of Christ. Then shall the Christian's longing for 'a calm and heavenly frame' be fully satisfied.

2. But the peace of God is also a *sentinel*: 'And the peace of God, which passeth all understanding, shall *guard* (*phrourēsei*) your hearts and thoughts in Christ Jesus' (Phil. iv. 7). The soul is no longer an arena, but a garrison ringed by battlements, posted within some high yet not impregnable castle. The sentry at the castle gate keeps watch. Who is he? Is he some warrior spirit, grey and stormbeaten, with face and form scarred with wounds? Is he some veteran, grim and terrible of mien, with an iron will and an iron heart? No, he bears no warrior's name. His name suggests no weapon and no strife. His name is—peace! Yes, peace is the protector spirit, the alert guardian, the watchman of our souls. Clad not in dinted armour but in white robes, mystic, wonderful, is this heavenly sentinel, the peace of God. When the Apostle adds 'which passeth all understanding,' he does not mean, as is commonly supposed, that this peace transcends all powers of human intelligence, every conception of human minds. But he means that the peace surpasses all human cleverness and device. Neither natural wit, nor skilfulness of resource, nor clear foresight can usurp the place of the peace of God and do for our inner life what it does. For within the garrison of the soul is a motley crowd of mutinous thoughts, of vain imaginings, of foolish and unholy desires. Can we, dare we take over the

guardianship of our thoughts, our whims and fancies? Are we able to give ourselves charge concerning our heart—so weak in its resolution, so wavering in its convictions, so ready to part with its best possessions, so quick to descend from its high ideals? We cannot ensure another's salvation, though we toil with unwearying effort and watch with tear-stained eyes; we cannot deliver another from sin or keep the tempter out, however tender and tireless our shepherding be. And we cannot unaided keep order within the citadel of our own soul. Take our thoughts—the thoughts of a single hour. What a strange phantasmagoria! Sordid, base thoughts succeed in a moment holy and beautiful thoughts. The sky of the soul is clear, when lo! the black cloud of evil desire sweeps over it and dims its purity. A shifting kaleidoscope of darkness and light, of love and hatred, of heaven and hell, is this inner world of a man's soul.

What power can drill this army of thoughts into order, into harmony with the Highest? What, indeed, but the sobering oversight, the tender yet stern dominance of the sentinel peace of God? Standing at our heart's gate, it is He that keeps the foe outside—the foe with ill suggestions of treachery and rebellion. It is He that pronounces the watchword before which the evil one sinks back ashamed and slinks into his native darkness. Nor is He our defender only. Within, under His watchful rule, the confusions and rebellions of the spirit settle down into resolute and calm obedience to the law of Christ. In *Paradise Lost* the gates of Satan's realms are guarded on either side by two formidable shapes, Sin and her offspring, Death, ' black as night, fierce as ten furies, terrible as hell.' There are many hearts that know no other warders; happy those whose inner life is guarded by the peace of God: for, as has been truly said, it is only ' over the slain body of the sentry ' that the forces of darkness and evil break through.

The Apostle further defines this thought by adding the words ' in Christ Jesus.' We could never be sure of the guardianship of the peace of God were it not for Christ. All the soul's joy and strength, all its power over sin, its inward freedom and serenity—these are the gifts of Christ. They are gifts which He enjoyed Himself in His communion with God; they are the gifts which He imparts to every soul in union with Himself. The peace guards our hearts and thoughts *in Christ Jesus*.[1] The great disturber of the inner life, next to sin, is *anxiety*. No more original, no diviner message ever fell from a teacher's lips than this ' *be not anxious for the morrow.*' St. Paul echoes it in this chapter: ' *in nothing be anxious.*' It is anxiety—the worrying forebodings, the fret and fever of depressing anticipation, of morbid fear—that clouds the spirit, that dulls its

---

[1] One of St. Paul's supreme phrases. ' The whole of Christianity ' (Westcott is reported to have said) ' hangs on the Greek aorist and the preposition *en*,' the ' in ' of the phrase which indicates environment, atmosphere, mystic union.

powers of service. The Christian needs to-day the serenity of Jesus, who left His life to be ordered by His Father, who lived each day as it came in the strength of His Father. Is the serenity of faith on the wane? Is it common to find a Christian who really casts his care upon God and cheerfully turns to the duty of the moment? Do we not let the current too easily carry us away—the current of calamity, of loss, of disappointment, of despair? Do we ever set ourselves to breast it bravely and to win new strength as we breast it? If we are to inherit the serenity of Jesus which failed not in the night of desertions, misunderstandings, and contumely, and which shrank not from the cross, then the peace of God, which guarded the citadel of His soul, is to be our sentry as well.

> Leave then thy foolish ranges;
> For none can thee secure,
> But One who never changes,
> Thy God, thy Life, thy Cure.

## CHAPTER II

## THE TRIUMPH-JOY

*Thanks be unto God, which always leadeth us in triumph* (thriambeuonti) *in Christ, and maketh manifest through us the savour of his knowledge in every place* (2 Cor. ii. 14, R.V.).

THERE is a remarkable richness and suggestiveness in the language of this doxology. The verb 'leadeth in triumph' awakens in the mind a host of subtle associations, which carry us back, on the one hand, to the beginnings of Greek tragedy in the *thriambos*, a hymn sung in honour of Dionysus; on the other hand, to the colour and movement of a Roman *triumphus*.

In his *Religious Teachers of Greece* James Adam has dwelt on the significance of that extraordinary drama, the *Bacchae* of Euripides. The play stands alone among the creations of a mind which for the most part shows itself in revolt from the national faith. Euripides is in effect the new theologian of Athens in the fifth century before Christ; but in the *Bacchae* he breaks into a vein of religious feeling or emotion, as if he were deliberately endeavouring to do justice to the inwardness and power of the mystery-element in the old Greek religion. Though the *Bacchae* may not amount to a recantation of a previous rationalism, it is at least the tacit acknowledgement of the potency of enthusiasm in the experiences of the soul. Nothing can be more sympathetic than his spiritualization of Dionysus-worship. The *motif* of the drama is 'The world's Wise are not wise.'[1] Dionysus is introduced to the conventional life of Thrace as 'a god of the wild northern mountains, a god of intoxication, of inspiration, a giver of superhuman and immortal life.'[2] His cult is intimately connected with certain forms of tree-worship, more particularly the vine. He is the wine-god, banisher of care and giver of peace.

It is well known that Orphism, which was really a revival of religion on mystic and emotional lines, and originated in the sixth century B.C., laid hold of the Dionysus-cult and transformed it. But in his portraiture of the Dionysus-worship, Euripides appears to go back to the primitive pre-Orphic setting of the faith, just as Sir Edwin Arnold, in his *Light of Asia*, reverts to the legendary sources of Buddhism. Now, the frenzy of the Bacchanal has its terrible side, as, e.g. in the tearing asunder and slaying of wild animals; while there is something revolting to the religious instinct of civilized humanity in the semi-sensuous fury of the whirling, dancing Mænad. But such phenomena take their place among the multitudinous expressions of religious enthusiasm familiar to the student of Comparative

[1] See *Bacchae*, 395.
[2] See Introductory Note to Gilbert Murray's translation of the play.

Religion; and Euripides undoubtedly brings out the nobler and more beautiful elements of the worship in those touches which emphasize the kinship with nature and the passion for personal purity characteristic of the god-possessed devotee. One may quote in illustration Professor Gilbert Murray's exquisite translation of one of the choruses of the *Bacchae* ('Some Maidens,' p. 53)

> Will they ever come to me, ever again,
>   The long, long dances,
> On through the dark till the dim stars wane?
> Shall I feel the dew on my throat, and the stream
> Of wind in my hair? Shall our white feet gleam
>   In the dim expanses?
> . . . . . . . . . . . . .
> O wildly labouring, fiercely fleet,
>   Onward yet by river and glen . . .
> Is it joy or terror, ye storm-swift feet? . . .
>   To the dear lone lands untroubled of men,
> Where no voice sounds, and amid the shadowy green
> The little things of the woodland live unseen.

Then follows a characteristic expression of the Euripidean faith or philosophy.

> What else is Wisdom? What of man's endeavour
>   Or God's high grace, so lovely and so great?
> To stand from fear set free, to breathe and wait;
> To hold a hand uplifted over Hate;
> And shall not Loveliness be loved for ever?

In the history of Christianity religious exultation has taken on many forms, fantastic and even grotesque, which remind us of the strange frenzies of pagan religions. One may mention the 'tarantism' of medieval saints, the levitations of some of St. Francis' followers, and the curious phenomena of Shakerism. That St. Paul recognized in the Christian joy a kind of intoxication is proved by his injunction to the Asiatic converts, ' Be not drunken with wine, wherein is excess; but be ye filled with the Spirit ' (Eph. v. 18). The Christian religion has a place for the *Gott-getrunkene*, the God-intoxicated souls; and it cannot escape us that the phraseology of St. Paul's ascription of praise in the passage before us recalls those earlier forms of religious emotionalism with which the exultation of the Christian saint may at least be compared, though its source is wholly different and its expression more ordered and self-controlled.

But the *thriambos* of Greece became the *triumphus* of Rome. The central object of Roman worship was the god Mars (Mavors, Marmor), and the most ancient priesthoods of Rome were consecrated to his cult. Among these—once more by way of religious analogy—we may mention the *Salii*—a band of youths who in the month of March performed a dance in honour of the god and accompanied it by a song. A litany has been preserved of the twelve ' Field Brothers '—the *Fratres Arvales*, a college dedicated to the worship of *Dea Dia*, the creative goddess—which curiously enough gives us the word ' triumpe ' as an exclamation of joy:

> Enos, Marmor, iuvato !
> Triumpe ![1]

[1] See Mommsen, *History of Rome*, E.T., i. p. 230.

## The Triumph-Joy

But the term was destined to express the celebration in pomp and splendour and processional magnificence of a great national victory. Was the Apostle moved to use the word by reflecting upon such a scene as that which is depicted on the bas-relief of the Arch of Titus at Rome? He did not, indeed, live to see that particular triumph into which were imported the spoils of the Holy City—the seven-branched candlestick, the golden trumpets, and the shewbread; but as a *civis Romanus* he would be familiar with the general features of the spectacle. The *triumphus* was granted only to a dictator, consul, or prætor, and in imperial times to the emperor alone, because the conquering generals were merely his *legati*. Let us imagine the streets adorned with garlands and the temples opened. The procession was headed by the great officials of the state and the senate, followed in order by the trumpeters, the captured spoils and trophies of the fight, the white sacrificial bulls, the prisoners spared to grace the triumph before imprisonment or execution, the musicians, and finally the general himself. '*Io triumphe*,' shouted the spectators, as the splendid pageant moved slowly up the Forum to the Temple of Capitoline Jupiter. There is a touch of the brilliant scene in the 'savour' of the Apostle's words. The air is filled with odours of spice flung around or burnt by attendants. In the only other passage where the verb occurs (Col. ii. 15), we read of Christ displaying the powers of evil like captives, or trophies in the procession, with the addition 'leading them in triumph'[1] on His Cross.

We pass from these side-lights on the history and meaning of the word and note that while the Colossian passage depicts Christ's triumph over His foes, the Apostle here conceives of God leading His subjugated saints in triumph, chained as captives to His car. Their defeat—the subduing of their rebellious passions and wills—is the secret of an abounding joy; for they share in the Conqueror's triumph, not as sullen, broken-hearted, and doomed captives, but as those who rejoice to be His prisoners and are proud to be trophies which grace His victorious might.

Further, let us note the 'always' and 'in every place'—expressions typical of the universal outlook of the Apostle whenever he deals with Christian experience. Times and places are all alike to him in the transcendentalism of his union with Christ. How closely he allies God and Christ in his thoughts here, as elsewhere. Whatever the environment of the Christian life, and wherever it may be lived, the source of joy lies in the fact that Christians are 'in Christ,' are so united with Him as to partake in the perennial gladness of His victory. The victory was won on the Cross: our victory over sin and self is involved in our crucifixion with Him—that identification of humanity with its Representative, by

---

[1] R.V. 'triumphing over them in it'; but there seems no good reason for varying from the translation 'leading us in triumph' which the R.V. gives in 2 Cor. ii. 14.

which the believing enter on the experience of forgiveness and inward peace. To St. Paul such a life as that which the saint lived 'in Christ,' was, so to speak, intoxicated with sheer vivid consciousness of His reality and power; or rather it might be likened to a triumphal march in the train of One, whom the author of the Epistle to Hebrews calls 'the author (or captain) of their salvation.' Out of it springs a fragrance diffused through the air invisibly interpenetrating the community — the 'fragrance' (*osmē*) that springs from 'the knowledge of Him.' To know Christ is to carry an aroma of beauty into the strifes and vulgarities of human intercourse. Flung back from the stress and strain of things, often discomfited and baffled and forlorn, we rest on that incommunicable *gnosis*, our apprehension of Christ. In itself, in its fulness, we may never be able to unfold it to others; but the 'fragrance' of it—the sweetness as of a hidden violet—is borne on the breeze and manifested in every place.

William Watson sings of the first spring skylark fluttering in the serene upper air and carolling in gladness above the vexed earth:

> O high above the home of tears,
> Eternal Joy, sing on!

But the Apostle felt a kinship with the divine joy, and a near fellowship with it in the midst of tribulation and perplexity. It was not something above him; but something inwrapt and indwelling in his consciousness. God 'setteth in pain the jewel of His joy.' And God was ever leading him in triumph with the great army of His saints. He stood not alone, but encompassed by a great brotherhood, 'a joy in widest commonalty spread.'

By this intoxication of spiritual joy, as if caught in the sweep of some world-wide triumphal progress, St. Paul is an exemplar for all time to the Christian who is apt to lose heart or faint in faith and prayer and hope. For with all the checks and drags upon its movement, the car of triumph, of Divine victory, still advances. When we centre our faith in Christ and draw from His teaching the eternal strength of wisdom and receive from His spirit the power that overcomes sin, God will verily lead us in triumph. There would be less pessimism, less concession to the secularism of the age, less falling away from a high ideal, if our hearts, like the Apostle's, were open to the potent assurances of the Divine joy, and we could feel through the air the measured march of the army of the living God in its steady triumphal progress to the ultimate victory of faith and righteousness.

## CHAPTER III

## A GOOD DEGREE

*They that have used the office of a deacon well, purchase to themselves a good degree* (1 Tim. iii. 13, A.V.).

AMONG the words of the Pastoral Epistles not found elsewhere, one of the most interesting is *bathmos*, which is translated 'degree' by the A.V. (following Wyclif) and 'standing' by the R.V. The word is found nowhere else in the New Testament. According to the Apostle a noble type of service in the diaconate secures a twofold reward—a stepping-place or vantage ground for further advance, and much boldness in the faith which is in Christ Jesus. Of these two resultant achievements we may leave the latter for subsequent treatment[1] and turn our attention to the former.

Undoubtedly the rendering 'degree' is a literal translation of the Vulgate *gradus* ('bonum gradum sibi acquirent'). 'Gradus' is a word which suggests a host of associations—ecclesiastical (e.g. graduale or service-book of portions sung *in gradibus* or on the steps of the choir) and scholastic (cp. Low Latin *graduatus*, which gives us our 'graduate'). The

[1] See Chap. vi.

'degree' which marks a distinct stage in a University career represents the Old French *degre, degret*, a 'step' or 'rank' (originally a step-down, as on a staircase). Murray (*Oxford Dictionary*, s.v. Degree) quotes Wyclif's quaint saying, 'Degre takun in scole makith goddis word more acceptable, and the puple trowith betere thereto whanne it is seyd of a maistir'; and for the meaning of 'step' he cites an illustration from Hakluyt (vol. i, 69), 'There were certain degrees or staires to ascend vnto it'; and the familiar words from Shakespeare's *Julius Caesar* (11, i, 26), 'He then vnto the Ladder turnes his Backe . . . scorning the base degrees by which he did ascend.'

The Greek *bathmos* is undoubtedly rendered quite correctly *gradus* in Latin, and 'degree' (=step) in English. It occurs in the Greek Old Testament more than once, evidently with this meaning, e.g. 1 Sam. v. 5, of the 'threshold' of the house of Dagon; 2 Kings xx. 9, of the 'ten steps' on the dial of Ahaz; and in Ecclesiasticus vi. 36, of the 'steps' of the door of the man of understanding ('if thou seest a man of understanding, get thee betimes unto him, and let thy foot wear the *steps* of his door'). This meaning is also well attested by examples in such writers as Strabo, Lucian, Appian, and Artemidorus.

While we speak of man of good *standing*, the Greeks, to represent the idea, used a word the etymology of which indicates movement and advance rather than rest and stationariness. If a deacon renders good service, his achievement instantly suggests further advance. But what kind of advance? It is certain that nothing can be further from the Apostle's thought than the idea of official promotion, or a rise in ecclesiastical rank. That indeed may be the result of approved fitness; but to make it a motive of service is very far from his purpose, and quite alien to his ideal. Hort, in his *Christian Ecclesia* (p. 202), interprets the term as 'a vantage ground, a "standing" (R.V.), a little, as it were, above the common level, enabling them (the deacons) to exercise an influence and moral authority to which their work, *as such*, could not entitle them.'

Undoubtedly faithful service lifts a man above his fellows and puts him in a position for exercising a wider influence: and this is true of the humbler and less conspicuous services of the Church. 'He that is faithful in that which is least, is faithful also in much.' But while the rise to a position of increased spiritual influence is assuredly implied by the Apostle's phrase, it is not a throne or seat of honour or eminence of which he speaks: it is a *step*; and a step implies advance, not mere elevation. It would be well, therefore, not to exclude the personal equation from the statement. Noble service secures a new foothold for further progress on the ladder, whereby we ascend to God. Tennyson has spoken of rising ' on steppingstones of our dead selves,' perhaps here following

Augustine's words, which have been so nobly interpreted by Longfellow:

> Saint Augustine! well hast thou said
> That of our vices we can frame
> A ladder, if we will but tread
> Beneath our feet each deed of shame.[1]

That is a different side of experience. The Apostle hints that the noble performance of a lowly duty is really an ascent of the *scala perfectionis*. Quite apart from its influence on others, the deed of love is a means of spiritual ascent for ourselves. Every conquest over slothfulness, self-absorption, and 'accidie' is to be regarded not negatively, but positively, as equivalent to the putting on of new strength and courage for the toils of self-sacrifice. The more we discover the inherent divinity of the obscure life when spent on the highest aims, the more fully are we encouraged to go on with it, to give up no noble quest, to surrender no high ideal. Each step in the steep ascent of the spiritual life is won by the patience of love: and each stage is the promise of the next. The Christian does not think so much of 'the world's great altar-stairs' as sloping 'thro' darkness up to God' (*In Memoriam*, lv); but rather, if he follow the thought of the Apostle, of an ascent into ever-clearer light, ever-deepening vision, of a progress in which abounding love girds him with nobler might and invigorates him with increased strength of purpose.

[1] See the poem entitled *The Ladder of St. Augustine*, which the poet bases on the words taken from the Third Sermon *De Ascensione*, 'De vitiis nostris scalam nobis facimus, si vitia ipsa calcamus.'

To the Apostle, therefore, the Christian service is not primarily the securing of a stable influence, the resting with satisfaction on noble achievements, the possession of a throne from which we can quiescently contemplate the flux and cross-currents of human life. Good work done is not a means to rest, but to further progress. 'If,' he exclaims, 'to live in the flesh—*if* this is the fruit of my work, then what I shall choose I wot not.'

The fruit of his work is the prolongation of opportunity. 'To depart and to be with Christ' is only 'far better,' because it will allow his energies to have fuller scope. With all his underlying mysticism, the Apostle was more Greek than Latin in his estimate of the Christian life. It was not so much *rest* within the Infinite that attracted him, as *movement* within the Infinite. The Western and medieval type of Christian thought was fascinated more by the idea of rest than of progress. Eternity with its serene Beatific vision, unclouded by the battles of time and its unaccomplished aims—this was the reward which dazzled the eyes of Augustine, Scotus Erigena, Bernard, Aquinas, and Dante. 'To the medieval thinker there was no great outlook upon time : no essential message of love was borne upon its stream save that very message which it had itself retarded and was still obscuring. The evil in the world must be fought against, but could never be exterminated ; it would, in some inconceivable manner, be transfigured to God and to His saints, but would never be annihilated to itself.'[1] But to the Greek type of thought, with which the modern world is more and more proving itself to be in sympathy, the problem of evil is not hopeless; nor does the universe bear upon it the marks of irretrievable failure. Our quickened sense of knowledge and of mastery over the forces of nature carries with it the unquenchable vision of progress. Alike in the moral and social sphere, the Christian life, while inwardly at peace with God, is outwardly a war against forces which cannot be finally impregnable. Evil, cruelty, injustice, hatred, vice—against these 'we fight to win.'

Through every grade and rank of Christian service, humble and unnoticed, conspicuous and public, there is to be seen the spirit of an unconquerable energy—unresting and unsatisfied, until the battle is won. There are moods of the soul when we cry:

> I do not ask to see
> The distant scene—one step enough for me.

But when the kindly Light has revealed the way and we have taken the 'step' firmly, let us move forward in the strength of what we have already attained, reckoning every advance in wisdom and love so much clear gain for that 'upward' calling wherewith we have been called by Christ, every fresh call to duty and service a 'degree' to be surmounted as the condition of our growth in the knowledge and grace of our Lord.

[1] Wicksteed, *Religion of Time and Eternity*, p. 32.

## CHAPTER IV

## FORBEARANCE

*Let your forbearance be known unto all men* (Phil. iv. 5, R.V.).

FEW words have given the translators of the New Testament more trouble than that rendered 'moderation' (*epieikeia*) in the Authorised Version. Archbishop Trench says, 'It has been rendered in all these ways : " Meekness," " courtesy," " clemency," " softness," " modesty," " gentleness," " patience," " patient mind," " moderation " ' ; and to his list we may now add the 'forbearance' of the Revisers (followed by Moffatt), as the latest attempt to fix its meaning. This is a formidable array of experiments, but the very multiplicity of translation gives a more helpful clue to the real meaning of the word than if we limited our view to the single rendering, 'moderation.' That expression, indeed, is slightly ambiguous. As interpreted by many, moderation does not rank as one of the heroic virtues. It stands for indefinite convictions. It smacks of compromise. The Laodicean, who is neither hot nor cold, is lost in the stirring strenuous movement of modern life. But this is not the moderation St. Paul commends. No prophet ever had firmer, more pronounced convictions than St. Paul, no teacher ever pressed home upon his followers more persistently than he the duty of loyalty to convictions. Witness his firmness in the grave crisis of the young Church, when he 'withstood Peter to the face.' A Laodicean attitude then would have checked the progress of a broad, catholic Christianity for years. Witness, too, his exhortation to his converts to cultivate steadfastness of faith, to quit them like men, to be 'no more children, tossed to and fro and carried about with every wind of doctrine.' He had no liking for the vacillating or tepid type of Christian character. Hence the popular idea of moderation as equivalent to loose-hanging principles finds no support in his writings. Those were days when men were fools for Christ's sake, and when faith crystallized in the storm of persecution. If the weak-kneed waverer did not develop strength in that bracing atmosphere, he withered as the hot-house plant shrivels when exposed to the frost. Nor in these days, when the tendencies that weaken religious convictions are subtle, many-coloured, insinuating, is there less need for deep-seated loyalty to the truths of conscience and revelation. We must ever distinguish between the large-hearted tolerance which consists with firm adhesion to principle, and the easy-going tolerance whose standards of judgement are shadowy and vague.

What, then, does the Apostle commend here? We answer, a rare and golden virtue, best understood, perhaps, if we glance at its opposite. Let us turn to that noble creation of the master-dramatist, *The Merchant of Venice*. Shylock the Jew will have naught but his pound of flesh. Insensible to mercy which 'blesseth him that gives and him that takes,' insensible even to an inducement on the lower plane of his grasping nature—the offer of money which would repay the loan twice over—he clamours for judgement and his bond. He is a stickler for his *legal* rights. His sense of justice, clouded by the spirit of revenge, narrows down to the bare letter of the law. On the other side pleads Portia with the eloquence of a noble magnanimity, setting forth how

> Earthly power doth then show likest God's,
> When mercy seasons justice.

St. Paul's *moderation* is nothing less than justice seasoned by mercy. It stands over against the justice which is hard, exacting, grim. It is the refusal to insist on our rights in those cases where the legal right becomes a moral wrong. Here let the grave Sir Thomas Browne take up the exposition: 'Let not the law of thy country be the *non ultra* of thy honesty, nor think that always good enough that the law will make good. Narrow not the law of charity, equity, mercy. Join gospel righteousness with legal right. Be not a mere Gamaliel in the faith, but let the Sermon on the Mount be thy Targum unto the law of Sinai.' In other words, Christian love steps in and corrects the justice that is unjust and the legality that is immoral.

The whole of Revelation shines with this light of forbearance. In the divine nature justice and love are eternally harmonized. Justice supplies the element of sternness without which love becomes weak sentimentalism. Love vouchsafes the gentleness without which justice becomes a relentless tyranny. For our view of God we must combine the teaching of Abraham's unavailing intercession for Sodom with the teaching of David's fall and pardon. We must associate with the parable of the barren fig-tree Christ's treatment of the woman taken in adultery. While God 'is slow to anger, and great in power, and will by no means clear the guilty,' He also 'retaineth not His anger for ever, because He delighteth in mercy.' In all His dealings with us we discern the unwillingness of infinite love to insist upon the rigid penalty of the law. 'All His goings back from the strictness of His rights against men; all His allowance of their imperfect righteousness and giving of a value to that which, rigorously estimated, would have none; all His refusals to exact extreme penalties'[1] are so many illustrations of that grace of *moderation* which the servant of God is in his turn to manifest towards 'all men.' Not only in the crowning act of redemption, but in each stage of human history and in the spiritual experience of individuals, 'He, who might the vantage best have took, found out the remedy.'

Now, when St. Paul speaks of the 'gentleness of

[1] Trench, *Synonyms of the New Testament*, p. 155.

Christ' (2 Cor. x. 1), he attaches the word to the Master, and thereby gives a clear call to the Christian. All who follow Christ have to imitate Him in this royal grace. For it was the divine patience of love that tempered the fiery zeal of the irritated disciples who were for calling down fire from heaven upon the churlish villagers; that made gentle response to the abrupt request of the practical and not too intelligent Philip, 'Show us the Father'; that, concentrated into a look, broke Peter's heart and roused him from the despair of his fall to that humbled, grateful service which he perfected in a martyr's death; that bore without reproach the unbelief of misguided but serious Thomas, and won him back to irrefragable faith. And outside the sacred circle, in His attitude towards captious scribe and Pharisee, towards rough Roman soldiers, towards the hungry crowds, towards social outcasts, towards 'all men,' we discern that gentleness which 'makes us great.'

We have all felt the temptation to play the part of the heated partisan who is blind to the excellence of an opponent's character, and acknowledges nothing in his point of view worth the slightest consideration; the temptation to take an unfair advantage of people we dislike in speech and action; the temptation to deal hardly with those in our power; the temptation to retort savagely on the rude speech of some ignorant but possibly well-meaning individual; the temptation to retaliate with unholy glee on one who has wronged us, and to bring him to justice without considering the provocation under which he acted or the punishment he has already brought upon himself and others. Sometimes we hesitate to make a concession which mercy, though hardly strict justice, demands, because we dread the imputation of weakness or the loss of a temporary advantage. Religious controversies, which are so often conducted without forbearance—the spirit of equity—shatter churches and provoke the scoff of the sceptic. We are not surprised to find that St. James, that great teacher of conduct, does not overlook this aspect of Christian character; for he speaks of 'the wisdom that is from above' as '*gentle*'; and it is notable that in the comparatively few passages where this spirit of 'sweet reasonableness'[1] is expressly taught, the epithet is comprehensively applied to those who to-day may appropriately manifest the virtue. For example, servants are exhorted in 1 Peter ii. 18 to be in subjection to their masters with all fear, 'not only to the good and *gentle*, but also to the froward.' In the discussion of the social problems of our day there is room for forbearance, that is, a more sympathetic appreciation of what constitutes the rights of others. The relations of employer and employed —to mention only one aspect of the social system— will only be permanently adjusted where the spirit of patient, mutual conciliation prevails. Forbearance

---

[1] Matthew Arnold's phrase in certain contexts is an excellent paraphrase of the Apostle's word.

is a pre-eminently social virtue. It is essentially brotherly. It softens hatreds. It breaks down class prejudices. It binds together the separated units of the community and erases the lines of demarcation in human life by insisting on a better understanding between man and man, and between class and class.

Likewise in the social life of the Church it has its recognized place. It is marked out as one of the virtues of a 'bishop' (1 Tim. iii. 3), who may be regarded as a typical church official: and of course it is applied to members of the church generally (Titus ii. 2). Who has not known of cases where the life of a whole church has been blighted by the uncompromising, self-opinionated attitude of some misguided official? Who has not heard of church meetings where the exhibition of party rancour, the interchange of personalities, the obstinate clinging to a pet detail—not to a large question of principle—has clouded the spiritual outlook for months and years, when some slight concession, some word of tact and forbearance, would have brought back sweetness and harmony? Neither for pulpit nor pew is forbearance a superfluity. When the orator Tertullus addresses 'the most noble Felix,' he invokes the 'clemency' (Acts xxiv. 4) which occasionally speakers in a better cause fail to win from fellow Christians. We know the type of hearer who settles down to listless indifference when his favourite preacher is not in the pulpit, or who 'damns with faint praise' the well-meaning but crude production of some pulpit tyro, or who only remembers a sermon from the fact that the preacher's diction was provincial. And we have heard of cases where the pulpit has been used for pointed reference to the faults of some objectionable individual, a member of the congregation, in a spirit of irritation or wounded dignity. It is evident that the resolute practice of social forbearance would bring a saner and purer atmosphere to many a church. We often pass judgements without thought of 'extenuating circumstances.' We do not make allowance for defects of training in the ignorant, or for the fight with temptation that precedes many a sinner's fall. Christ saw 'with larger, other eyes,' the hearts of men. He was never 'coldly sublime, intolerably just,' in presence of weakness, failure, sin. While the guilty, in face of His divine purity, were abashed as they realized the heights from which they had fallen, they also felt that divine love was stooping from the highest heaven to lift them out of the mire. There are some sins that God tolerates in us so long as we do not tolerate them ourselves. There is something juster than legal justice.

## CHAPTER V

## REDEEMING THE TIME

This striking phrase occurs in Col. iv. 5 and in Eph. v. 16. It is a mark of Pauline style to close a sentence with a pregnant participial clause which lends emphasis and richness to the preceding words. In both passages the phrase is connected with an injunction referring to the Christian's 'walk' or, as we should say, his daily life: but in the Colossian passage the reference to daily life is restricted so as to particularize the Christian's influence on those who are without,[1] an idea which reminds us of 1 Tim. iii. 7, where the Apostle, in discussing the qualifications for the office of bishop, says he 'must have a good report of them who are without.' The Christian must stand well with unbelievers outside the circle of the Church: he must also ever keep them in view, so far as the influence of his personality is concerned. It should further be noticed that the Ephesian passage, which is more general in its application, adds as a reason for redeeming the time the words 'because the days are evil.'

Now, what does the Apostle mean by redeeming the time or the opportunity (*ton kairon exagorazomenoi*)?

[1] See *inf.* Chap. ix.

In the first place, it is well to recognize that there is a difference of opinion with regard to the translation of the verb 'redeeming.' Lightfoot on Col., *loc. cit.*, renders it 'buying up for yourselves'; but Armitage Robinson on Eph., *loc. cit.*, remarks that we have no evidence for regarding the word as equivalent to the Latin *coemo* ('buy up'), and that the general usage of St. Paul (cf. Gal. iii. 13, iv. 5) points to the meaning 'buying away from' = redeeming, but not (he adds) in the sense of making up for lost time, as in the words 'Redeem thy misspent time that's past.'[1] The days are evil: the present has got, so to speak, into wrong hands: the Christian must purchase it away from these misusers. The Vulgate gives us *tempus redimentes*; and we may paraphrase the Apostle's meaning thus—claim the present for the best uses. If the days are evil, that fact only adds point to the nobler use of time. If those who are without are to be won, each moment as it arrives must be employed for the great ends of the kingdom of heaven.

In the second place, we have to establish the meaning of *kairos* the word rendered 'opportunity.' Doubtless it is more than once used by St. Paul (cf. especially Rom. iii. 26) as practically synonymous with the general word for time, *chronos*;

[1] The correct and original form of the line in Bishop Ken's famous morning hymn. The variations 'Thy precious time mis-spent redeem' or 'Redeem thy mis-spent moments past' are to be reckoned as examples of the unnecessary and often unjustifiable practice of altering the original wording of hymns. Sometimes the authors, but more frequently hymn-editors, are responsible for the changes.

## Redeeming the Time

but it is a mistake to overlook its proper signification of time in the sense of opportunity or the fitting moment for action; and, indeed, the cases are rare where the context does not suggest, however faintly, a specific occasion or portion of time. It is the condition of the age ('the days are evil'), or the condition of the unbelieving world, that suggests the present as an opportunity to be purchased without delay and invested in the noblest service.

There is an illuminating passage in Butcher's *Harvard Lectures on Greek Subjects* (see pp. 117-120) where that brilliant interpreter of the Greek spirit draws out with convincing force, as well as subtle intuition, the distinction between time viewed in its extension or succession of moments, and time 'charged with opportunity.' The transformation of Chronos, the slow-moving, silent, almost inert teacher, revealer, and agent into Kairos, the youthful keen, determined aggressor, is characteristic of the Hellenic genius. 'Chronos remained on the whole too abstract, too indeterminate, to admit easily of personal embodiment in literature or art. It was otherwise with Kairos, a word which I believe has no single or precise equivalent in any other language. Kairos is that immediate present which is what we make it: Time charged with opportunity, our own possession to be seized and vitalized by human energy, momentous, effectual, decisive: Time, the inert, transformed into purposeful activity.'

All this is borne out, as Butcher proceeds to show

by the representation of Kairos in art and literature. Ion composed a hymn on Kairos, in which he is called the youngest child of Zeus : opportunity being conceived of as the latest and God-given gift. In art he is represented in the guise of Hermes, as wrestler or charioteer, swift but sure in decision. 'Sometimes he is a youth pressing forward with wings on his feet and back, holding a pair of scales, which he inclines with a slight touch of the right hand to one side. His hair is long in front and bald behind : he must be grasped, if at all, by the forelock.' In one relief he is contrasted with Regret (*Metanoia*), 'who is a shrinking and dejected form, standing beside an old man symbolizing the sadness felt over the last moment which cannot be recalled.'

It is not surprising that the conception of Kairos, which thus possessed the Hellenic imagination, should have passed over into the language and thought of Christianity. In the Wisdom Literature of the Old Testament, which is the outcome of the contact of Hebraism with Hellenism, the idea of the right time for action, as dictated by motives of common sense or expediency, or revealed by observation and experience of life, is frequently expressed. 'To everything there is a season' (Eccles. iii. 1). On this passage Dr. Moffatt (*Literary Illustrations of the Bible*) quotes Thomas Fuller : 'He is a good time-server that finds out the fittest opportunity for every action. God hath made a time for everything under the sun, save only for that which we do at all times—to wit, sin.' And this comment reminds us that the Christian view of life is characterized by a spiritual urgency which never appears in the literature of wisdom or philosophy. Indeed, there is a silent and subtle transformation of the old conceptions and language in the Christian environment, whereby we become conscious of entrance into a new order of thought. From the Christian standpoint life is not less purposive and active than in the Hebraic and Hellenic philosophies; but it is transfigured by new motives and ideals connected with the unseen. The doctrine of the Divine Fatherhood sanctifies human responsibility; it carries with it an ethical ideal, 'We must work the works of Him that sent Me, while it is day' (John ix. 4); the works of the Father—grace, compassion, love—these are impressed on His children as a divine duty.

Hence Kairos, interpreted in the light of the mind of Christ, looks less at self and more at humanity. Its watchword is not so much success as salvation. The Cross, as Matthew Arnold pointed out (*St. Paul and Protestantism*, p. 75), is not an appeasement of God's wrath, but a death 'to the law of selfish impulse,' which had corrupted the heart of mankind. Jesus suffered not for His good but for ours: His death was a 'witness' to self-effacing love: it was also a 'ransom' in respect of our need.

We have yet to proceed on the spirit and virtue of the Cross. 'The days are evil' because the Spirit of the Crucified who suffered not for His own need but for ours, has not prevailed over the inherent, self-regardingness of human hearts. The Nietzschean 'will to power,' the Darwinian 'survival of the fittest,' the common, worldly-wise principles of 'getting on in the world,' all point to an individualistic conception of opportunity which easily harmonizes with human impulse. Christianity, on the other hand, with its basic concept of the solidarity or brotherhood of the race, regards time as an arena of self-sacrifice, where each life in its own way, by its particular ability and influence, gives a contribution to the ultimate 'kingdom of heaven.' 'If,' in effect says the Apostle, 'time is imprisoned in the sphere of self-seeking, buy it back: ransom it from so ignoble and deadening a scheme of life, and your walk will be with Christ.' Redemption of the present, then, is bound up with the Christian view of life as a self-realization which is possible only through self-abandonment. 'Walk in wisdom toward them that are without, redeeming the time.'

No doubt these thoughts may seem to carry with them an ideal 'for earth too high,' to proclaim a kind of disregard of personal success and ambition, and to exalt a spiritual passion which may appear to leave the ground 'to lose itself in the sky.' When one remembers how many thousands are living a hard life, employing a mediocre ability in an endless struggle to keep their place; how many thousands also, through the mere stress of life, and in particular lack of employment, have lost all ambition and initiative—it might seem more fruitful to appeal to the natural instincts of self-preservation and self-aggrandizement; to call on the multitude to look after self and ignore their neighbours, to proclaim a kind of *sauve qui peut* in the general confusion of things : but this way lies madness and the degradation of mankind. Christianity proclaims the duty of individual activity, self-improvement, the cultivation of our gifts and tastes, the perfecting of every power, and it thereby condemns indolence, paralysis of will, inertness of despair, and drift. But to redeem the time is to consecrate our character and capacity to the kingdom of God; to make our goodness a contribution to the world's happiness; to learn every day how useless and sinful are ingratitude and sullen hopelessness, how much better it is to be kind to people than to stand on our rights or to be haughty and harsh-tempered, how it is possible in thousands of little ways, in every sphere, to cultivate considerateness and charm of manner, how much nobler it is to encourage the best in others by avoiding the spirit of malice and the language of irritation, and 'so to collect about us' (as Stevenson says) 'the interest and love of our fellows, so to multiply our effective part in the affairs of life that we need to entertain no longer the question of our right to be.'

## CHAPTER VI

## BOLDNESS OF SPEECH

*Having therefore such a hope, we use great boldness of speech* (2 Cor. iii. 12, R.V.).

IN a discussion of the ' good degree ' (1 Tim. iii. 13), we noted that a further achievement of a nobly-fulfilled diaconate was ' much boldness (*parrhēsia*) in the faith which is in Christ.' The word is not less interesting because it is a very familiar term in the Apostle's vocabulary and indeed in the New Testament generally. The deacon learns the value of a joyous fearlessness of utterance in matters of ' the faith,' the faith which lives, and moves, and has its being ' in Christ.' Even more striking is the passage above quoted, where the Apostle is contrasting the old order and the new, the old with its ritual which kept God at an awful distance and veiled His glory, and the new with its freedom of action and access and movement for the soul. 'Where the spirit of the Lord is,' cries the enthusiastic Apostle in memorable words, ' there is liberty.' And liberty is the atmosphere in which boldness of speech blossoms like a white rose of the garden amid the pure airs of the countryside. Neither word, indeed, is specifically Biblical. Plato, in the *Republic* (557 B), brings the two together in his discussion of a democracy: 'Does not liberty of act and speech abound in the city?' But there is a peculiar beauty and power in the words when brought into relation with the *civitas Dei*.

Boldness of speech is a term which Christianity has borrowed from classical Greek only to invest it with a new and more glorious meaning. Indignation might drive a Juvenal into verse; but it is a full heart, conscious of the richness and transforming energies of a new evangel, that moves the Christian to frankness of speech. We use great 'plainness of speech' is the familiar and delightful A.V. rendering. The Vulgate is here somewhat colourless, and gives us *fiducia* as its rendering. This is a case which illustrates the truth of Bishop Westcott's saying, 'Latin is all angles: but Greek has no angles at all.' And he went on to quote *Verbum caro factum est*, protesting against the inadequacy of subject and verb. *Fiducia* hardly conveys the idea of boldness of *speech*. The fact is, Latin cannot give us an equivalent for the term. The boldness of Peter and John (Acts iv. 13) is wrongly translated *constantia* (Vulg.); for what the priests and elders marvelled at was not so much the courage of Peter and John, but the fine boldness of their oratory, the surprising eloquence of 'unlearned and ignorant men.' This, however, is what the first enthusiasm for the gospel produced. One of the gifts of God enumerated by Clement (1 Cor. xxxv. 2) is 'truth with boldness,' truth openly and plainly declared, without economy or obscurity similarly, in the epistle to Diognetus xi. 2, we have the expression, 'with boldness speaking' indicating the clearness and intelligibility of the gospel. But the Apostolic Fathers do not use the word so freely as the New Testament writers. Sometimes we ask ourselves whether the New Testament writers mean to express by the word the candour which leaves nothing obscure or unintelligible; or the boldness which utters the truth and the whole truth: probably both ideas are conveyed in the word, and the exact *nuance* has to be caught from the context. The word certainly is contrasted in John xvi. 25 with 'parable, and means there, as in John x. 24, 'clearly' and 'unambiguously,' *ohne Umschweife*, as Preuschen[1] puts it. But in St. Paul's Epistles we get passage after passage, like Eph. vi. 19, where the word undoubtedly indicates that right of free speech which as Lightfoot remarks (see note on Phil. i. 20), is the badge, the privilege of the servant of Christ.

We may note in passing that the author of the Epistle to the Hebrews (cf. iii. 6; iv. 16; x. 19, x. 35) appears to broaden out the meaning, as when he says, 'having therefore *boldness* to enter into the holy place,' and, 'let us draw near with *boldness* to the throne of grace'; but it may be doubted even in such passages whether the word really loses its connotation of speech or the utterance of words. Freedom of access to God goes along with

[1] See *Handwörterbuch zu den Schriften des Neuen Testaments*, 1910, *s.v.*

freedom of speech: both are gifts of 'the better covenant.'

With these facts before us, it may be relevant to ask the question, is boldness a characteristic of modern religious life? Both our Lord and His Apostles place a remarkable emphasis on our powers of speech and conversation, not only because of the temptations and perils that beset us in this form of self-manifestation, but mainly because they knew that the language of the lips was an all-important element in the Christian service. 'By thy words thou shalt be justified, and by thy words thou shalt be condemned.' We publish ourselves not only in our set utterances, but in the casual table-talk and conversation of our daily lives. For the most part we avoid direct allusions to religion, its vital experiences and claims. Often this is due to a healthy hatred of unreality and cant, often to a feeling that reticence best befits matters of sacred import and all intimate concerns of the soul. But there is a grave danger lest we should go too far in this cultivation of silence, and lose that gift of buoyant and natural testimony which entered so largely into the early life of Christianity. Christianity had nothing to conceal, though her enemies made much of her secret meetings and strange rites. 'Come and see' was always her invitation to the questioning mind. The *disciplina arcani*—the reservation of truth for the few initiated—is alien to her spirit, and Tertullian was a mistaken exponent of the religion which he sought to defend, when he stated that Christians could not on evidence reveal the mystery of the Lord's Supper.[1] 'The truth as it is in Jesus' was spread by the testifying powers of the 'saints,' servants of Christ who indeed were far from perfect but were yet conscious of the mighty change He had wrought in them. Commenting on the lives of the early Methodist preachers, A. Caldecott[2] made the following statement: 'Religion is for the race and not for the individual soul (only): the flow of spiritual grace seems impossible where the habit of reticence prevails. I cannot but ascribe the wide range of Methodism in the Christendom of to-day to its conviction that the bearing of testimony to the realities of the spiritual life is perfectly natural in itself, and a means by which the Holy Spirit extends His grace from soul to soul.' It is not every one that has the authentic gift of testifying; but how few professing Christians ever realize that the practice of boldness of speech is too easily neglected? The power is latent in every true Christian heart, though for reasons of temperament, natural shyness and diffidence, it may never come to development. There are Christian men and women who (to quote Alexander Maclaren) 'can talk animatedly and interestingly of anything but of their Saviour and His Kingdom.' Why? Because their hearts are not full. 'The real reason for the unbroken silence in which many Christian people conceal their faith is mainly the small

[1] See Gwatkin, *Early Church History*, i. p. 188.
[2] See Caldecott, *The Religious Sentiment*, p. 4.

quantity of it which there is to conceal.' Undoubtedly, the secret of the Apostolic outspokenness lay in the fact that they were men full of their subject: the tongue became eloquent because the springs of their being had been reinforced by a new Divine energy. They were emancipated too: 'delivered from the bondage of corruption into the liberty of the glory of the children of God'; and their first instinct was to declare their joy. As Charles Wesley puts it in one of his hymns:

> What we have felt and seen,
> With confidence we tell,
> And publish to the sons of men
> The signs infallible.

And similar outpourings of souls, 'disburdened of their load,' find expression in the characteristic hymns of Methodism.

Another element in the frank utterance of the Apostles, especially of St. Paul, was the passion for the souls of men. They spoke the winged words of conviction, of warning, of persuasion, of strong faith and fiery love, because they felt the infinite peril of the ignorance, darkness and degradation of the society in which they moved 'as luminaries, holding forth the word of life.' Their one desire was so to speak as to arouse in the hearts of their hearers a sense of sin, and to give them thus awakened a vision of Christ.

> Oh, could I tell, ye surely would believe it!
> Oh, could I only say what I have seen!
> How should I tell or how can ye receive it,
> How, till He bringeth you where I have been?

> Therefore, O Lord, I will not fail nor falter,
> Nay, but I ask it, nay, but I desire,
> Lay on my lips thine embers of the altar,
> Seal with the sting and furnish with the fire.
> (Myers' *St. Paul.*)

It is perhaps the thought of a fruitful service of witness-bearing, free from the taint of self-seeking, which inspires St. John, in one of the two passages of the Epistles (1 John ii. 28; cf. 1 John iii. 21) where he uses the word to say, 'And now, my little children, abide in him: that if he shall be manifested, we may have *boldness*, and not be ashamed before him at his coming.' If we are to carry our free unreserved utterance over into eternity, even into the Presence of the Judge and not shrink from Him 'like guilty things ashamed,' it will be on account of the brave witnessing for the truth to which both the Giver and the Gift of the gospel inspires every single-minded and self-effacing servant of Christ.

## CHAPTER VII

## EARNEST EXPECTATION

THE interesting word (*apokaradokia*, Vulg. *expectatio*) translated by A.V. and R.V. ' earnest expectation ' is found only in two passages in the New Testament—both in St. Paul's writings (Phil. i. 20, Rom. viii. 19). In Phil. i. 20, it is linked with the familiar 'hope,' in order to lend emphasis and intensity to the Apostle's characterization of the forward-looking element of his spiritual experience. He is speaking of the proclamation of Christ as a source of personal joy; and this immediately suggests the part he himself can play in the magnifying of his Master. His whole being throbs with the glory of the prospect that stretches before him like a fair landscape; and he exults in the passionate hope that he will know no shrinkings of shame, but rather break into a glad abandonment of holy boldness in the preaching of Christ—' whether by life or by death '—in that body, which has been absolutely devoted to this sacred service.

The word itself, etymologically considered, suggests two ideas; first, awaiting with outstretched head; second, diversion from other objects (cf. Hastings' *Dictionary of the Bible*, 'Expectation'). The preposition *apo* (as in *aphorōntes*, Heb. xii. 2, ' looking *away* from everything else to Jesus '), conveys the idea of concentrated attention; the other components—'head' and 'watch'—express the physical manifestation of eager expectancy in the head bent forward, e.g. to catch the first glimpse of the advancing pageant or procession in a street. One finds oneself on a railway platform bending forward to get the first view of the oncoming engine, as it rounds the edge of a curve which shortens the vision of the line. This is expectancy of the outstretched head.

It is, however, in the second passage referred to above, namely, Rom. viii. 19, where the word is used with expressive power, owing its peculiar appropriateness to the context of the Apostle's argument. Indeed, the problem to be solved is not its exact meaning, which is hardly in doubt, but the implication of the word 'creation' (*ktisis*). What is 'the creation,' which is in a state of vivid expectancy, waiting with a kind of tense impatience for the manifestation of the sons of God? Is it inanimate Nature, or the universe regarded as a whole? Are not the limitations of time shared alike by Nature and Man? Is not the wound from which creation suffers, and under which it groans with the painful sense of imperfection, a wound that affects not only the physical environment of human life—the fabric of the natural world—but also the spiritual being of mankind? Without doubt the word 'creation' is almost invariably used *physically* in the Old Testament and Apocalypse, but the context of such New

Testament passages as Mark xvi. 15, Col. i. 23, implies 'a special reference to mankind as *the creation*' (see *Dictionary of the Bible*, 'Creature'). While no doubt the effects of human transgression are conveyed to material things and all nature may properly be said to share in the sense of a destiny inchoate and incomplete, of a glory temporarily forfeited but eventually to be realized, it is especially the sentient creature that the Apostle has in view when he thus speaks of an expectant world.[1]

For, quite apart from the philosophic consideration that the so-called emotions of objective nature only owe their validity to the self-consciousness of man, quite apart from the fact that only in the human spirit arises that conception of an immanent divine life which is the ground of our belief in a rational universe, it is the interpretative, responsive soul of man which most truly is conscious of the state of imperfectness so graphically described by the Apostle in this passage. Some of the older commentators would assign the spirit of earnest expectation only to regenerate man. But there is nothing to show that the Apostle is dwelling at the moment on the distinction between man as regenerate and unregenerate. It is of course true that the experiences of the saints and of the unrepentant denote very varying degrees of spiritual sensibility. The saint looks forward to

---

[1] But see on this passage Rom. viii. 19, Sanday and Headlam (*International Critical Commentary*), who repudiate Origen's interpretation of 'creation' as the world of man.

the 'far-off divine event' of a spiritualized humanity with a positive conviction and intensity, which are foreign to a soul fast bound in weakness and sin, and incapable by its very hardness of cherishing such an ideal. But is it not true that, negatively, even unregenerate man in his deepest emotions is conscious of a broken and defeated existence, that he, too, in some sense is dimly looking out to a better destiny, to a new world of moral strength and purity which will replace the dark, narrow region in which he has hitherto moved?

In most philosophies and in the best literature of the past we are everywhere met by evidences of the deep-seated weariness of the human heart 'moving about in worlds not realized,' and hungering for the solution of the riddle of existence. But in the New Testament we discover that this sense of infinity stands in a new setting and is interpreted from an original standpoint. 'The manifestation of the sons of God'—the issue of that sifting process whereby a new spiritual humanity shall come into being—remained in ancient thought a dream. But the person of Christ to such thinkers as St. Paul, St. John, and the unknown author of the Hebrews, supplied the key to the mystery of life. He was the bringer-in of a new order, the founder of a new humanity. Those who found life in His name received 'a spirit of adoption'—became conscious of a new relationship with God, of an inward witness that sealed on them the spirit of sonship. The conception of sonship opened up the vista of a new inheritance, theirs only, because already Christ's. What did it matter if they suffered *with Him*? They would eventually be glorified *with Him*. Earthly suffering was naught compared with the glory to be. The whole creation was now thrilled with a vast hope. It was this hope, whereby the sons of God realized the true experience and the full meaning of salvation. They were verily saved by hope. They could not be blind to the fact that their own experience was the sign of a universal purpose ' to deliver creation itself from the bondage of corruption unto the liberty of the glory of the children of God.' Their self-consciousness became transfigured by a world-vision, by a vivid expectation of a final manifestation of God's sons. We know from St. Paul's statements elsewhere how this hope triumphed over the facts of racial distinctions and separations. Nothing in the outward universe could weaken its power. Only within was its real enemy to be found: its enemy was to be found in the limitations of bodily existence, its weakness and its pain, its depressions and its sicknesses. The body had yet to be redeemed: the sons of God themselves groan under the pressure of its thwarting and paralysing infirmities. Yet even in the region of corporeal imperfection the divine hope cannot be quenched. It lives on as ' the master light of all our seeing.'

Thus the Apostle, under the inspiration of Christ, thinks—believes and hopes—in universals. The

Church has still to rise to the splendid universalism of his thought. But is the average member of the Church on the tiptoe of eager expectation? Is his life being enriched and 'enthused' by the world-hope of the manifestation of God's sons in all the nations and empires of the world? The 'earnest expectation' of the saint is the crown, the full splendour of that yearning that flickers and falters in the hearts of mankind. The world on the whole, marches to the strains of futurity; but it is the Christian who knows best what the 'unveiling,' the real 'apocalypse,' is to be: he views the progress of the race and the issues of life and destiny that are slowly being shaped in the evolution of humanity, he views all with the perspective of Christ. In those wonderful lines written on Tintern Abbey, Wordsworth contrasts the conception of nature, wrought within him by experience, with that which he cherished in his earlier years:

> More like a man
> Flying from something that he dreads, than one
> Who sought the thing he loved.

But now all is changed:

> For I have learned
> To look on nature, not as in the hour
> Of thoughtless youth; but hearing oftentimes
> The still, sad music of humanity.
> Nor harsh nor grating, though of ample power
> To chasten and subdue.

And withal there is the 'sense of something far more deeply interfused,' the indwelling spirit of the universe. A similar enlargement of vision, whether as regards humanity or God, accompanies the growing apprehension of 'the mind of Christ.'

With the same facts before them how vast a gulf separates St. Paul from Marcus Aurelius! Listen to the noblest of the later Stoics—the philosopher-emperor—' Up and downe, from one age to another, goe the ordinarie things of the world, being still the same. And either of everything in particular before it come to passe, the minde of the Universe doth consider with itselfe and deliberate: and if so, then submit for shame unto the determination of such an excellent Understanding; or once for all it did resolve upon all things in general: and since that, whatsoever happens, happens by a necessary consequence and all things indivisibly in a manner and inseparably hold one of another. In summe, either there is a God, and then all is well; or if all things go by chance and fortune, yet maist thou use thine own providence in those things that concerne thee properly: and then art thou well' (ix. 28, Casaubon's trans.). Surely Pantheism never produced a serenity so grave and virile; but contrast that view of the Universe with the Pauline conception of a Divine Love ceaselessly at work to deliver creation from corruption, to enlighten, redeem, and renew human nature, and to inspire His children with the hope of a supreme Consummation—the final triumph of righteousness.

It is the unfaltering optimism and the noble hope begotten in his heart by Christ that enables him to say, 'The earnest expectation of the creation waiteth for the revealing of the sons of God,' and to add, 'If God be for us, who can be against us?'

## CHAPTER VIII

## SINCERITY

FOUR times in the writings of St. Paul there appears the clear shining of a virtue of exceeding purity and whiteness. It is the virtue of sincerity (*eilikrineia*). Here are three of the passages: 'Let us keep the feast . . . with the unleavened bread of *sincerity*' (1 Cor. v. 8); 'In holiness and *sincerity* of God . . . we behaved ourselves in the world' (2 Cor. i. 12). 'As of *sincerity* . . . speak we in Christ' (2 Cor. ii. 17). Thus sincerity chastens with its refining grace the communing soul in the great Christian feast. It casts its hallowing light upon the common concerns and the daily conduct of the saint in the world. It is the crystal spring from which wells up undefiled the speech of the Christian teacher. Lastly, it is a crowning beauty of that spiritual wisdom which has been taught of love 'to discriminate the things that transcend.' For the Apostle with eagerness anticipates, as one of the fruits of the spiritual life of the church at Philippi, this result—'that ye may be *sincere*' (Phil. i. 10).

The root-idea of sincerity abounds in the New Testament: but the particular word which St. Paul uses in these texts is so picturesque that it stamps itself at once upon our thought. It is picturesque, whichever of the two most favoured etymologies we adopt. One theory derives the word from the process of testing by sunlight[1]; as if, for example, one should hold up a piece of paper to the light to discover its marks or its flaws, or to assure himself of the purity of its workmanship. Another theory is that the word is really a strategical term, and is derived from the distinctive companies into which an army may be divided: thus it signifies distinct and unmixed, like a body of troops wearing the same colour and uniform. These, then, are the possible shades of meaning in the Apostle's word—open to the light, sun-tested, or pure and harmonious throughout. Who does not covet a 'conscience as the noonday clear'—a character of such translucent texture that it can endure to be scrutinized in the rays of the Sun of purity? We are pitifully conscious that there is so much in the best of us, and in our best, that cannot face the light. Who does not long for an outer life which moves in harmonious line with our truest self, not swerving from the behests of the inward Guide, following with rhythmic step His high commands? Do we not feel too often a lack of what we may call inevitableness in conduct—a need of firm and definite outline in word and deed? To be a trimmer, a 'double-minded' man, a servant of two masters—that way lies spiritual incompetence. To speak and to act in unhesitating obedience to the

---

[1] This derivation is supported by Moulton & Milligan, *Vocabulary of the New Testament*, s.v.

## Sincerity

law of conscience, to the voice within—this is the mark of Christian sincerity. Such are the notes of this great virtue which we may briefly consider—to keep our hearts open to the light of holiness—to be so uniform, so pure in life that none can mistake or distrust us.

1. To be sincere, then, is to be able to endure the light without shrinking or distress. The light—that which is true and valid for us—may vary with the individual vision, but one is taking the upward path whose master light is the highest, the best known to him. Let a man bring his inner life to the illuminating rays of the Best. Let him investigate his duty, his daily task, his common habits by ' the gleam, the light that never was, on land and sea '—the unseen Truth that is truth for him: and he takes sincerity for his friend. Says T. H. Green [1]: ' By " sincerity " (*eilikrineia*) is to be understood, I think, perfect openness towards God: that clearness of the soul in which nothing interferes with its penetration by the divine sunlight. Given this openness on our part, Christ, the revealed God, will gradually find His way into our souls, not in word but in power.' It is true that this light summoned as the test of character blinds and scorches. ' Thou hast set,' says the Psalmist, ' our secret sins in the light of Thy countenance.' ' Who among us,' echoes Isaiah, ' shall dwell with the devouring fire ? Who among us shall dwell with everlasting burnings ? ' and he is thinking of no

[1] *Two Sermons,* p. 41.

future fires, but the ever-present, encompassing blaze of the divine Righteousness. The angel in Newman's *The Dream of Gerontius* says to the soul in its upward journey to the beatific vision:

> Learn that the flame of the everlasting Love
> Doth burn, ere it transform . . .

The guilty Sir Lancelot, bursting into the high tower where lay the Holy Cup, is burnt and blinded by the flare as of a furnace.

> O, yet methought I saw the Holy Grail,
> All pall'd in crimson samite, and around
> Great angels, awful shapes, and wings and eyes;
> And but for all my madness and my sin,
> And then my swooning, I had sworn I saw
> That which I saw: but what I saw was veil'd
> And cover'd: and this Quest was not for me.[1]

But this is the discipline by which the soul's deep insincerity is shown up: this is really the 'cleansing fire' from which the soul emerges repentant, purged from the glamour of the false, converted in its best self to the true. The judgement day is always here. The Judge is ever on the throne. Insincerity loves secrecy and hates publicity. It shrinks from the light of judgement and cares not to be unmasked. 'Every one that doeth evil hateth the light, neither cometh to the light, lest his deeds should be reproved.' Yet, however painful such self-investigation may be, it is the first step to 'the life that is life indeed.'

Dante in the *Paradise* describes how at length he

[1] Tennyson, *The Holy Grail*,

*Sincerity*

saw the Rose of God, the glory of the Deity, and this is his experience:

> Such keenness from the living ray I met
> That if mine eyes had turn'd away, methinks
> I had been lost. . . .
>
> It may not be
> That one who looks upon that light, can turn
> To other object, willingly, his view.
> For all the good, that will may covet, there
> Is summ'd; and all, elsewhere defective found,
> Complete.[1]

From this point of view it becomes a sheer joy for the Christian to walk in the light, to be permeated with God. Turn where we will, we find His rays. To quote T. H. Green (*ibid*. pp. 42-3): 'In great books and in great examples, in the gathering fulness of spiritual utterance which we trace through the history of literature, in the self-denying love which we have known from the cradle, in the moralizing influences of civil life, in the closer fellowship of the Christian society, in the sacramental ordinances which represent that fellowship, in common worship, in the message of the preachers through which, amid diversity of stammering tongues, one spirit still speaks—here God's sunshine is shed abroad without us. If it does not reach within the heart, it is because the heart has a darkness of its own, some unconquered selfishness which prevents its relation to Him being one of " sincerity and truth ".'

In so far as we absorb ' the Light of the World '

[1] *Paradise*, Chap. xxxiii. 76-9, 100-6 (Cary).

by contemplation and by faith, do we seek for truth in the inward parts. We will hate our sinfulness, as we mark it in the all-revealing splendours of His purity, and we will purify ourselves 'even as He is pure.'

2. To be sincere is, furthermore, to preserve an unbroken harmony between one's words and deeds and our deepest inward convictions. We have to be to others what we are to ourselves. There is a wide distinction between being 'all things to all men' and a hard Machiavellian diplomacy. The one has unselfish ends and is the tact of love; the other is essentially a policy for selfish ends. Quick changes belong to the shifting scenes of a play. In the open air of reality we have to dare to be ourselves, and not to adapt our convictions to our environment. We have to allow no tricks of manner, no affectations to disguise our truest self. To act a part which we do not feel, to conceal the truth under a polite insincerity, to keep silence so as to give a wrong impression of our opinions, to depreciate ourselves when we are secretly proud of our gifts, to state a half-truth because it is popular and will be cheered by the gallery, 'to assume a virtue if you have it not'—these and a thousand others are the ways of the insincere. The worldly-wise Polonius was for the moment inspired when he said:

> To thine own self be true,
> And it must follow, as the night the day,
> Thou canst not then be false to any man.

## Sincerity

The subject of hypocrisy in religion at once suggests itself, and our Lord's unmeasured denunciations of the Pharisees rise before us. He had compassion on the sinner—the man who, though bad, did not cloak his badness; he was severe on the professor of righteousness, whose heart was unloving. His scathing invectives stand out alone in the gospel narrative. They were the most terrible words that fell from His gentle lips. In what did the hypocrisy of the Pharisees consist? We do not understand Christ's attitude until we can answer the question. It was the want of harmony between the inner and the outer life that moved Him to indignation. Witness His comparison of the Pharisees to 'whited sepulchres, which outwardly appear beautiful but inwardly are full of dead men's bones. Even so ye also outwardly appear righteous unto men, but inwardly ye are full of hypocrisy.' They were guilty of both simulation and dissimulation—of being what they were not, of not being what they were. They were simply actors. There are hypocrites in every walk of life, but hypocrisy is a marked thing in the sphere of morals and religion. It stands out sheer and conspicuous against the white background of high and holy professions. The world gives it short shrift. It is a false note in the most glorious of symphonies—a hopeless blotch in a picture of beauty. Christianity is the living of a true life—can never be the acting of a part. Its atmosphere is alien to all insincerities, which are swiftly detected, like artificial flowers set in the sunshine of a garden by the side of the living rose and the breathing violet. Of love and faith—two of the great graces of the Christian life—the Apostle says of the first that it is to be 'without dissimulation,' and to the second he appends the word 'unfeigned,' which is exactly the same epithet, and may be translated 'unhypocritical.' So St. James, that prince of ethical preachers, speaks of the wisdom that cometh from above as 'without hypocrisy.'

It is in language—written and spoken—that insincerity is ever the patent flaw, sincerity the supreme desideratum. The note of sincerity is sadly missing in much modern and popular literature; and there is a morality of style which is not often discussed or even recognized, as Dr. Dale points out in his lectures on preaching. 'For truthfulness of speech it is not enough that we never say what we know to be false; we must do our best to form a style that shall be an accurate expression of our inner thought and life.' But in everyday life how familiar, how rarely condemned, how often palliated, how almost mechanical is insincerity of speech! It takes forms of flattery, false modesty, exaggeration, formality. It is fulsome and 'damns with faint praise,' pays homage that is not meant, hides behind a specious cordiality a secret dislike, raises expectations that are never fulfilled, and makes promises never meant to be performed. It is Protean in its mannerisms, shifts, disguises and shapes. In literature the personification of this spirit is Goethe's Mephistopheles and the hateful Iago, who by hints destroys the virtue of the innocent and the trust of the lover. But not only from the tragedies of *Faust* and *Othello,* but from all our experience of life do we learn how sincerity is one of the pillar virtues, because it supports a whole fabric of trust and friendship. If the pillar snaps, the fabric is wrecked. Terrible indeed is the nemesis of insincerity. It stands solitary and gaunt—a ruin among ruins. Its fate is loneliness—not the loneliness of the moral hero or the martyr, which is glorious—but the loneliness of sin at length found out, of falsity unmasked, which is the 'outer darkness.' This is perhaps why the Apostle links with the word ' sincere,' as if in explanation, another phrase, ' and void of offence.' The purity of the Christian character is not unfrequently a refuge for the battling and defeated multitude—a covert from that tempest, before which they are weak and driven. When such purity fails, there is one refuge less for the helpless.

' If therefore the light that is in thee be darkness, how great is the darkness ! '

> When the lamp is shattered,
> The light in the dust lies dead.[1]

And in the dust, too, will lie the faded love and faith of those who have been disillusionized by insincerity.

[1] Shelley, *Lines* (1822).

## CHAPTER IX

## A GOOD REPORT FROM WITHOUT

WHEN St. Paul, writing to Timothy, advises him to select for the office of 'bishop' one who, among other qualifications, 'must have a good report of them which are without' (*apo tōn exōthen*, 1 Tim. iii. 7), he suggests an important and oft-neglected test of Christian character. We cannot afford to depreciate or ignore the estimate formed of us by those who have no association with the Christian Church. Looking at the matter from the standpoint of the progress of religion in the world, the clear, definite type of the Christian character as set forth by individual members of the Church of Christ is of immense moment, when we remember that in every sphere of life the majority of people have little or no personal experience of the religion of Christ. Those who are 'without' may be active opponents of the truth, or they may be simply indifferent, or they may be keeping their minds in suspense. In any case, if they come to form respect and admiration for a true Christian, wherever he may be found, their testimony is all the more cogent by reason of the hostility or indifference or suspense out of which it has been created. The reluctant admiration of the foe is a more impressive

## A Good Report from Without 73

witness to the reality of religion than the amiable applause of a mutual admiration society. The general whose experts had given a unanimous opinion as to the safety of a certain fortress would be confirmed in his acceptance of this opinion if he happened to learn that a spy from the enemy's camp had pronounced the position impregnable. A man may be a model of all the Christian virtues in the eyes of the small religious coterie of which he is a shining light, yet to the world in general he may be extremely objectionable. We may make due allowance for the bias with which the world's verdict is weighted; still, a man may well examine himself if he discovers that his influence on those who are outside is next to nothing, whatever it may be within the Church. On the other hand, when the verdict of the world coincides with the verdict of the Church, he becomes a factor in the progress of religion.

It is folly to suggest that the outsider is not in a position to judge true Christianity. That is to take the professional religious view of man as totally and absolutely depraved. It is the view which Christ condemned, not only by His spoken words, but by the methods of His ministry. For He proved in scores of cases that the spirit of good was not dead in the churchless, the worldly minded, or the vicious. Under the influence of a divine life and a divine sympathy the instincts of holiness revived in the sinner, and he stood on the threshold of the kingdom of heaven. We may take it for granted that the world is not so far alienated from God as to fail to recognize in the spiritually minded the divine impress.

> Oh, we're sunk enough here, God knows! but not quite so sunk that moments,
> Sure tho' seldom, are denied us, when the spirit's true endowments
> Stand out plainly from its false ones.[1]

When the worldly man secretly adores the Christian, envies his peace, covets his nobility, he condemns himself, and at the same time the latent divine life stirs within him. It is a humbling consideration to most Christians that they fail to evoke this responsiveness to the high and holy which lies hidden in so many careless hearts. We may protest that it is illogical for the crowd to form its judgement of Christianity from defective Christians. Doubtless it is so, but the fault does not lie solely with the crowd. The standard of judgement will alter when the reformation has begun from our side. It is obvious that immense impetus would be given to the energies of the Christian Church if those who are without could be led to admit that a rare and peculiar beauty shines in the Christian character. The distinction of character which might be supposed to mark off the professing Christian from the world in general is often hazy and intangible. If there is special religious earnestness without a corresponding elevation of character, the criticism is ready to hand that this is a case where a man's sympathies run to religion just as another's run to photography or science or sport.

[1] Browning, *Cristina*.

Spirituality sinks to the level of an emotional eccentricity in the opinion of the cynical.

Surely for our own generation the ethical test of the Apostle is not an anachronism. Never was there an age in which it was more necessary to insist that those who have passed through the spiritual experiences of conversion and regeneration should stand out with a certain distinction of character. There are some lines in Wordsworth's *Prelude,* of which Coleridge remarked that he would have cried, ' Wordsworth ! ' if he had met them running wild in the deserts of Arabia. If we may compare great things with small, the Christian character must be instantly recognizable as unique, original, distinguished. The Christian is to be what Christ intended him to be, like ' a city set on a hill, which cannot be hid.' The workmanship of the divine Architect must be clear and conspicuous. The saint must tower, like Saul, above the crowd ; but, unlike Saul, he must tower by virtue of his moral stature, beauty, and power. And wherever this nameless charm, this ' beauty of holiness,' this distinctiveness of Christ-like qualities is marked, men will say—it is the only explanation possible to them— ' This man is of that " city, which cometh down from God out of heaven ".' The peculiar creed to which we may give our faith, or the ecclesiastical organization in which we have been trained, is nothing to the world. The fact of association with the Christian Church may be only a symptom of social respectability. The supreme thing is the type or mould of our moral and spiritual being. The sect is nothing ; the character is everything.

There is yet another standpoint from which we may view the estimate of the outsider; for the Apostle adds as a reason for his test, ' lest he fall into reproach and the snare of the devil.' In other words, if the Christian, whether in official connexion or otherwise with the Christian Church, is badly reported of those who are without, it is not only a reproach to his religion, but it is a grave menace to his own spirituality. Failure to impress the outside world with the divinity of our character will sooner or later result in our taking the world's view of our religion, as a factor unreal and ineffectual in our moral being. No one goes down so quickly as the man who has lost caste. The penalty of a tarnished reputation is moral recklessness. When that mood settles down on the soul, Satan, the crafty hunter—so picturesquely limned for us by the Apostle's closing phrase—spreads his toils in anticipation of an easy prey. The verdict of those who are without reacts upon those who are within ; and the hold we have on spiritual realities slowly relaxes under the icy blast of contempt. The reproach of the outsider places in peril the soul of the Christian who has been a hearer, but not a doer, of the word ; and it sooner or later reveals the foundation of sand on which he has built.

Hence the impression we leave upon others inevitably corresponds with the impression which Christ leaves upon us. Like the monogram inscribed on a seal, which is not to remain as a mere decoration, but is to be communicated to the documents we attest, so the stamp of the divine image must not lie dormant, unused within us, but must be impressed on the tablets of many human hearts. If the impress of Christ upon our souls has been faint or fleeting, our character becomes a vague, ineffectual witness of His love. But given that divine sealing which marks him as the Master's own (2 Cor. i. 22), the influence of the Christian is cumulative, definite, assured. His growth in the knowledge of his Master is growth in the power of penetrating and uplifting the careless, hardened, despairing souls of men. He will make real to others the Master who is so real to himself. He will bring a new vision of Christ to many to whom Christ has only been a blurred, indistinct figure, hardly descried through the mists of their prejudice, self-will, and carelessness. 'The human lineaments' will 'shine irradiant with a light divine,' as on the Mount of Transfiguration, when the clouds vanished and the disciples beheld 'Jesus only.'

## CHAPTER X

## THE UNATTAINED IDEAL

THE passages of St. Paul's writings, in which he speaks in the first person, are of lasting value. They are fragments of spiritual autobiography. Gathered together, they make a series of 'confessions' unequalled in the history of saintliness. Here is one: 'Not that I have already obtained, or am already made perfect; but I press on, if so be that I may apprehend that for which also I was apprehended by Jesus Christ' (Phil. iii. 12, R.V.).

1. We have in the last clause the starting-point of all spiritual advance: 'I was seized by Christ.' That arrest by Christ is the vital fact of his experience. It not only diverted the course of his life, it remade the man. He fell into complete captivity to the personality of Christ. Christ entralled his will, his inner consciousness. That is the beginning of a new life, the *fons et origo* of Christian manhood.

2. He has been arrested for a supreme object—an ideal life, of which he gives no definite account: he can only say 'that for which I was seized by Christ Jesus.' As a matter of fact, St. Paul knew perfectly in its general features the new life that Christ had enabled him to undertake. It was a life of 'faith on the Son of God,' a life of *koinōnia,* communion

## The Unattained Ideal

with Christ, but a communion issuing in the service of love. If he died with Christ, he rose also with Christ: but that inward crucifixion and resurrection was not a mystic 'experience' unrelated to his outward conduct: it was the very spirit of self-surrender, which flowed through his deeds and made them pure. Nevertheless, in detail he will not characterize the attainments of the holy life. Here his language is less definite, even vague. He had set foot within a sphere whose distances were infinite, whose borders no man knew. That is one of the supreme notes of Christian experience, distinguishing the new life of faith from the old life of works. In the life of works there was finality. 'As touching the law blameless,' he could say of himself. He might have echoed the young ruler's words, 'All these have I kept from my youth up,' with his eye on the requirements of a merely external code. But now he was face to face with a larger law, a nobler vision. The life of Christ was a life of heavenly, far-extending horizons, a life in which all attainments, however good, seemed but the prophecy of something better, a spiritual progress of which finality was not to be predicated.

3. Out of this conception of the Christian calling emerges naturally his view of 'Christian perfection.' There is a sense of the word 'perfect' (*teleios*) which St. Paul might have applied to himself. As a matter of fact, he did so. In a succeeding verse (see verse 15, 'Let us therefore, as many as be perfect,' &c.) he

actually classes himself among the 'perfect.' And rightly so. He is no longer a babe in Christ: he has a fullness of knowledge and vision belonging to mature or full-grown Christian manhood. But simply because he has reached this stage in his spiritual development, he cannot speak of himself as having already obtained or as being already *made perfect*. The very perfection or completeness of his knowledge means an enlarged sense of what Christ requires. He could not think of any state of Christian experience which meant finality or the ceasing of effort, in which he need no longer consider himself as a sinner or without limitations. There can be no state of holiness in which a man may be supposed to have reached an independent or self-contained life. The essence of holiness is dependence. Hence his idea of what has been called ' Christian perfection ' is that of an ever-deepening communion with Christ, a love of God which is supreme, ' with all his heart, and with all his strength, and with all his mind ': but not a state in which he can think of himself as already perfected, nor one in which his daily efforts to do God's will have ceased. Expressed in this way, no one can fail to believe in this high type of Christian grace. It is when we find people professing to be ' perfect ' with no consciousness of shortcoming or failure that we must fain protest. This is not New Testament teaching, nor the teaching of experience. The greatest saints—the ' perfect ' of the Christian Church—have always been conscious of deficiency. In that respect human experience offers no analogy to the consciousness of Christ. His holiness involved no sense of failure or sin. He is sublimely unconscious of fault or of the need of penitence. It can never be so with His followers; their saintliness is in essence a growing consciousness of imperfection. Professions of special saintliness are ever perilous. The most potent and entrancing forms of the saintly life are those in which there is no consciousness of special grace or holiness. Like Moses, they wist not that their faces shine: yet their lives are irradiated with a beauty that cometh down from above.

4. Finally, we have the Apostle's plan of life—'I press on.' I am always in pursuit—pursuit of the gleam. But the gleam is ever in front, is ever receding. In the spiritual realm ideals are not attained, nor attainable. Fruition is not of the life that now is. The life that now is, however noble and strenuous, leaves us with a pitiful sense of incompleteness. It is a fragment—a broken arc. Yet the incompleteness of life, the unattainableness of ideals, is the very condition of progress. We are saved from despair by the thought that we are potentially perfect, 'complete in Christ.' The actual perfection shines on in front of us, beckoning us upward to higher things. And there lies the practical value of a doctrine of holiness or a high standard of spiritual life, a standard which quickens flagging energies, breaks up self-complacency, rouses from

disillusionment, and calls on us perpetually to 'press on.' What of the average Christian life? Is this mark of apostolic grace on it? Do we not look in vain for the stress and strain of mighty spiritual effort? Are not most Christians content with themselves as they are? It may be that a former age laid too much emphasis on the saving of our souls, and dwelt too analytically on the state of the heart. But we have swung to-day to the opposite extreme; we consider it to be a refined selfishness or a subtle species of hypocrisy to cultivate the spiritual life in its richer aspects, to labour anxiously up the steep sides of the Mount of God. Yet it was in such saints of old that the love of humanity and the passion for souls came to its perfection. Read Augustine's *Confessions,* and remember that when the Roman Empire was falling into decay under the barbarian invasions, this mystic, introspective thinker, by his conception of the City of God, quickened within the Church a sense of unity and inherent grandeur which saved it from sharing the fate of the empire, and enabled it to rise into a stable, rock-like institution, against which the gates of Hades could not prevail. Read Wesley on *Christian Perfection,* and remember that this preacher of inward holiness was the evangelist that saved eighteenth-century England. These were the men who, perpetually drawn upwards to the higher realm, above an ever-lessening earth, yet by that very ascent were quickened into new zeal for perishing humanity. The world to-day fixes a keen,

## The Unattained Ideal

critical eye on the Church of Christ. And what does it see in the average Christian, the church-going professor of Christ? It sees him apathetic and comfortable, conventionally good, easily sinking into a dull, respectable and decorous religion. And then it recalls the Apostles passionately and eagerly laying their gifts of holiness and love at the disposal of a dark and dead world. Or it recalls the Founder of Christianity, and remembers His 'secret'—the taking up of a cross, the losing of life in order to gain it. And it reverts to the ordinary Christian, without passion for the spiritual life or the regeneration of his fellows; and compares him, not to the eagle that soars upward to the sun, but to the sea-bird that flutters contentedly in the sand-ooze left by the ebbing tide.

This is doubtless a biassed verdict, and not the whole truth, but nevertheless it touches on a weak element of modern Christianity, or at least of many a Christian life—the absence of an overwhelming, compelling, spiritual ideal. 'A man's reach should exceed his grasp, or what's a heaven for?'—so says Browning in his marvellous estimate of Andrea del Sarto. The artist painted in a style of cold, faultless perfection: and yet his unerring precision, flawless and admirable though it was, represented a fettered soul that had forfeited the larger vision. Others, so far as mere technique were concerned, could not approach him: their products were rougher, less finished; but yet there shone in their work the colour and sweep and majesty of the great design, the glorious ideal, that atoned for all defects of workmanship. Is not that the lesson for the Christian of to-day? Is he not too easily satisfied with the life of cold, correct, and decorous obedience? Is there not absent alike in his aspirations and attainments the warmth and richness of a great purpose? What is wanted is a revival of spiritual idealism—or, to put it more simply, a revival of enthusiasm. Oh for the eagerness, the entrancing vision, the ceaseless spiritual effort of the Apostle! Nothing short of this can make Christinity a force in the modern world, and without it the Christian Church cannot win humanity for the kingdom of heaven.

## CHAPTER XI

# BONDS AND THE UNBOUND WORD

*My bonds became manifest in Christ throughout the whole prætorian guard* (Phil. i. 13. R.V.).

*I write this letter to you in prison bound with chains, and expecting on the morrow the sentence of death, yet fully trusting in God that I shall not swerve from His truth nor swear denial of the errors, whereof I have been charged by false witnesses. What grace God hath shown me, and how He helps me in the midst of strange temptation, you will know when by His mercy we meet in joy in His presence.*

John Hus *to the people of Bohemia* (June 10, 1415).

THE imprisonments of Christian saints have almost invariably 'fallen out rather unto the progress of the gospel.' What heroism and patience have been begotten by bonds! What noble literatures have issued from the gloom of lonely confinement! What sublime inspirations have emanated from the souls of Christ's bondsmen in all ages, to startle a careless world and to rekindle the dying fires of faith! Listen to Cyprian writing in the third century to his brethren in the mines: 'They have put fetters on your feet and bound those blessed limbs and temples of God with vile chains, as if the spirit could be bound with the body. . . . O blessedly bound feet, which God shall release! . . . O feet, delaying in fetters for a

little; but soon to run the glorious course to Christ!
... Not with pillows and couches is the body
cherished in the mines, but with the comforts of
Christ. Wearied it lies on the ground; but it is not
pain to lie down with Christ.'[1] Of course, this is
but an example on the wider field of history of what
is true in the individual experience of the followers
of the Crucified. The light affliction worketh for us
more and more exceedingly an eternal weight of
glory. God employs the limitations and distresses
of His people for His own high ends. Martyrdoms
are never lost: they are the foundation of churches.
Persecutions scatter the faithful abroad only to extend
the Kingdom elsewhere. The seeds of truth are
borne on the wings of the tempest to other soils. For

> behind the dim unknown
> Standeth God within the shadow, keeping watch
> above His own.

No more striking expression of this fact is to be
found than in the verses from which the quotation at
the head of this chapter is taken. There are touches
and hints in them which might easily escape the
unimaginative and careless reader. But relate them
to all that can be gathered of the circumstances of
St. Paul's imprisonment, and they are instantly
luminous with charming significance. First of all
we gather that his imprisonment has one supreme

---

[1] Quoted from Cyprian, Ep. 76 (in H. O. Taylor's *Classical Heritage of the Middle Ages*, p. 210). See for further illustrations Workman's *Persecution in the Early Church*, Chap. v.

result. His bonds have become manifest as being
'in Christ.' Whenever we light on this memorable
phrase in Pauline writings, let us pause. Here is the
man's experience and faith and theology—his universe
of ideas compressed, as it were, into a single yet all-
comprehensive formula. To be *in Christ* is his daily
life. To be *in Christ* is his working creed. To be
*in Christ* is his enduring hope. All he cares about is
that his whole activity shall radiate into earth's
darkness this glorious fact. And to at least one
section of the secular powers of Rome he, a prisoner
of the empire, gives unmistakable proof that he is no
mere political or treasonable offender against imperial
law. He has not violated the *lex maiestatis*. He is
simply the firm, unswerving, pertinacious friend and
adherent of one Christus, a dead prophet of the
province of Judæa. That he, an obscure Jew,
should have been able not only to prove his innocence
to the military camp of Rome, but also to have
flashed into that charmed circle the mysterious name
of Christ, is an achievement which only a prisoner of
his Master could have accomplished. St. Paul the
prisoner does a more extraordinary thing for Christ
than St. Paul the free could have done. How does
this come to pass?

St. Paul is not immured in a state gaol. He is 'in
his own hired house.' But he is nevertheless a state
prisoner, guarded constantly by a soldier. To his
sentinel he is bound by a chain that encircles his
wrist. The probability is that his warders were told

off for this duty in a regular succession. Certain it is that they were all drawn from one body, the famous prætorian guards (*praitorion*).[1] These guards, the creation of Augustus, were destined to play a momentous and tragic part in the history of the empire. Originally about ten thousand in number, they were increased under Vitellius to sixteen thousand. They were intended to support the person of the emperor against the encroachments of the senate or in the event of a public revolt. They were stationed in a permanent and strongly fortified camp to the east of the Quirinal and Viminal hills. As Gibbon characteristically remarks, 'In the luxurious idleness of an opulent city their pride was nourished by the sense of their irresistible weight, nor was it possible to conceal from them that the person of their sovereign, the authority of the senate, the public treasure, and the seat of the empire were all in their hands.' It was, then, from this famous circle of the Imperial lifeguards that St. Paul's warders came. This gave him an opportunity, which he eagerly seized, of planting Christianity in the heart of the military forces of the empire.

Consider, however, the daily trial to the prisoner involved in this peculiar custody to which he was subjected. Even if the prætorian were of a kindly and sympathetic nature, it would jar upon a sensitive spirit to be constantly overlooked and to feel that every word and tone were the object of a curious

[1] See Moulton and Milligan, *Vocabulary of the Greek Testament*, s.v.

supervision. How much more so if the man were a coarse *miles gloriosus,* brutal and a braggart withal, like most of his order! But St. Paul allowed no personal annoyance or hardship to quench his zeal for Christ. If ever he felt the irksomeness of the situation, that feeling would be instantly subordinated to the sense of its responsibility. Here he was each day brought into contact with every type of human character, with complex and varying phases of the human soul, with many grades of moral deficiency and ignorance. Here he was to meet the pagan deadness to righteousness, the contempt of all emotion, the apathy to all but the animal side of life. But the Roman always respected courage and endurance. A failure of temper and patience on the part of the prisoner would have been fatal. St. Paul was for the time being an element of novelty in the monotonous prætorian experience. He became a fascinating theme. He was invested with the attraction of an unexplained mystery. Was he reminded by the fetter on his hand that the succession of the guards meant a chain of testimony of which each soldier was a new link? 'Had he only sometimes,' says Moule,[1] 'only rarely, only once or twice failed in patience, in kindness, in the quiet dignity of the gospel, the whole succession of his keepers would have felt the effect as the story passed from one to another.' But he did not fail, and his bonds became manifest in Christ throughout the prætorian guard.

[1] *Philippian Studies*, p. 50.

There was a further element in the situation. St. Paul was not without visitors. Sometimes he was refreshed by the kindly, cheerful presence of a friend like Onesiphorus. Sometimes he had to engage in a solemn and earnest conversation going right home to the innermost facts of the soul; probing a dull, dead conscience like that of Onesimus the runaway slave, who had drifted to Rome from far-off Colossæ only to sink to the dregs of the city rabble until, by a miracle of grace, he found out St. Paul, and the prisoner becomes his saviour. Occasionally, as we know from the Acts, St. Paul had conferences with the Jews, 'to whom he expounded the matter, testifying the kingdom of God, and persuading them concerning Jesus both from the law of Moses and the prophets, from morning till evening.'[1] The prætorian stood in the background during these conferences. He might be impressionable, or blasphemous, or scornfully argumentative, or utterly indifferent. It is difficult to realize how the truths of the Christian faith would make their way into the consciousness of these rough, untutored men. Probably the personality of St. Paul would appeal to them most. He might seem at first to be merely a setter forth of strange gods or a fanatical exponent of a new legend of deity; but they would soon discover that he was a man of robust and attractive mould, a type of nobility new and fascinating in the prætorians' experience of their fellows. And his personality

[1] See Acts xxviii. 23.

commended his creed. Into the ranks of the imperial troops for the space of over two years the gospel of Christ penetrated with its mysterious and perhaps only partially realized message—a message sealed upon the interest of the camp by the wonderful prisoner called Paulus. To his greatness there was an unbroken testimony; and it was through his greatness that the new truth, which was eventually to become the religion of the empire, was now beginning to make itself felt.

But while in one direction the bonds of St. Paul became a pioneer agency, a propaganda of the truth as it is in Jesus, in another they acted as a wonderful stimulus to the courage and fearlessness of the 'brethren'—the Christian community, which, if we may believe Lightfoot, was even then a large body in the city of Rome. They rely on or trust in his bonds, we read; and the expression is remarkable. For the bonds of a prisoner whose fate still hung in the balance might seem to be but a poor foundation for confidence. Nay, his imprisonment might rather suggest a sense of insecurity and doom to Christ's followers in the city. On the contrary, the heroism of the Apostle became to them a new assurance of the goodness and ultimate victory of their cause. They beheld in him a true, 'happy warrior,'

> More skilful in self-knowledge, even more pure,
> As tempted more; more able to endure
> As more exposed to suffering and distress.

This was an element in the Christian character

which was destined to impress Roman emperor and Roman populace alike with a new sense of human dignity. The Christian played the man with adversity. He touched the instincts of nobility more effectually than the Stoic, as his strength was tested more severely than the Stoic's. Bonds, fires, lions, tortures, the cruel death of the amphitheatre—none of those things moved the Christian. Though, as Matthew Arnold says, ' deep weariness and sated lust made human life a hell ' in those days of decadent civilization, still the Roman clung to life as the only certainty he knew. He marvelled to see men part with their lives cheerfully for the sake of an unknown god. Christianity advances through heroism—the heroism that is obedient even unto death. Nothing breaks up the apathy of a worldly world like a cross voluntarily, joyously, bravely endured. Men of the world are conscious of strange, fierce heart-searchings as they look on a Damien dooming himself to a certain death, bidding farewell to life and pleasures and friends, shutting out the world to spend and be spent for Christ among the lepers of Molokai. We are not called to suffer for our faith to-day like the heroes of old. But heroism is still demanded. The cross has still to be borne. Is a high-wrought, luxurious civilization enervating the Christian character? Are we less inclined to endure hardness for Christ's sake? Is the Church failing for want of heroes? Is it true that often those who take life's ills most calmly stand outside the Christian Church, and by their unfaltering courage rebuke the followers of Christ ? Listen to a modern singer :

> Out of the night that covers me,
> Black as the pit from pole to pole,
> I thank whatever gods may be
> For my unconquerable soul.[1]

This is the Christian spirit divorced from the Christian creed. But the most lasting and most potent factor in the regeneration of the world is the love that is born of the constraining love of Christ. The heroism that falls upon the thorns of life and bleeds, yet rises again and pursues unflinchingly its noble quest, is contagious. It is a transfiguring force. It is the inspiration which makes men ' more abundantly bold to speak the word of God without fear,' while it draws the waverer and the despairing and the sinful into the serried army of the Lord.

[1] W. E. Henley, *A Book of Verses*, p. 56.

## CHAPTER XII

## ENDURANCE

One of St. Paul's favourite words is endurance (*hypomonē*) which is invariably rendered by 'patience,' its Latin form, in the Authorised Version. It occurs at least a dozen times in his letters, while when the substantive is used as a verb, it is found triumphantly adorning the attributes of Love in the great Hymn with its characteristic touch of universalism in the sentence: 'Love endureth all things' (1 Cor. xiii. 7). In the apocalyptic passage of St. Luke xxi. 19, it stands out as a saving virtue: 'in your patience ye shall win your souls' (R.V.). St. James, who attaches the quality to Job (v. 11), stamps it with his approval in his opening words, 'the proof of your faith worketh patience, and let patience have its perfect work' (i. 3, 4).

Now this word, which we prefer to render 'endurance' so as to preserve its identity in the use of the verb 'endure' ('patience' has no corresponding verb in English), is not to be confounded with another beautiful word, likewise a favourite with the Apostle Paul, namely 'longsuffering' (*makrothymia*). The distinction between the two is admirably set forth by Lightfoot (Col. i. 11): 'while *hypomonē* (endurance) is the temper which does not easily succumb under suffering, *makrothymia* (longsuffering) is the self-restraint which does not hastily retaliate a wrong. The one is opposed to *cowardice* or *despondency*, the other to *wrath* and *revenge*.

'Longsuffering' is by St. Peter applied more especially to God. 'The longsuffering of God' waited in the days of Noah (1 Pet. iii. 20 and in 2 Pet. iii. 9), that same longsuffering is the means of man's repentance and later is in effect man's salvation (*ibid.* iii. 15). But with St. Paul it is one of the fruits of the Spirit as associated with the forgiving nature which is essential alike to a right relationship with God and our fellow men (Gal. v. 22). But endurance is an essentially human virtue, like humility. It is called into play by the manifold conditions of our life on earth. Humility indeed stands out in the first Beatitude in the phrase 'poor in spirit' as expressive of the Christian temper in its estimate of the real values of life. The spirit of the Western world is often here in contrast with that of Oriental minds. A Hindu is more naturally attracted by the Franciscan type of Christian practice with its voluntary choice of poverty than by that of the average Englishman who appears to be arrogant rather than humble-minded, but he will be ready to admit the latter's quality of endurance, the faculty of cheerful acceptance of unpleasant conditions, of sticking things out and carrying on with the duty in hand, however distasteful or monotonous.

Apart from the Christian standpoint, the capacity

to hold out amid soul-fretting conditions of our daily work, the work allotted to us and sometimes the reverse of what we would have chosen for ourselves, is a secret not only of success but of happiness, but when this virtue is sublimated by a consciousness of duty to God,

> Who fixed thee mid this dance
> Of plastic circumstance,
> This Present thou forsooth would fain arrest,

then we understand better what a powerful factor it becomes in the development of the Christian character. Endurance is not the cultivation of a facile optimism, but of a cheerful hopefulness born of the sense that our life is not a blind alley but a probation for something greater and far better. It was said of Rosebery by one of his friends that he was among those who like the palm without the dust. It is, of course, the toil that matters and gives value to the prize, but for the toil the quality of endurance is essential. When we look at our daily work we sometimes imagine we shall break under the strain, for so much of it seems merely mechanical and gets us nowhere:

> To-morrow and to-morrow and to-morrow
> Creeps in this petty pace from day to day . . .

Often it is true that we fail in our aims but we never fail to win something if we endure. Even a genial humanist like the Roman poet Horace sang the praises of 'the upright man tenacious of his purpose.'

He was touched by the Stoic ideal to which St. Paul himself owed not a little, but the Apostle's scheme of existence was learnt from Christ. Not to lose heart when all seems against us, not to yield to craven fears, not to give up striving even if the fulfilment of our hopes and the achievement of our aims seems nebulous, is hard for average humanity. Nevertheless, it may be a God-appointed discipline. Suppose everything came easily to us, wealth, promotion, fame, success, we should be getting what we desire without a struggle. Yet by escaping the dust it is possible to lose the prize: for the prize is our own character. Nothing else matters, and if we evade the struggle or slacken effort, we miss the discipline which makes us what we have it in us to be. Our personality is in this life to be tested by 'temptation,' a word whose application we need not limit to enticement of evil, but which is to be extended to every kind of test to which our soul is to be subjected.

Apart from our life-work, there is the service of others, an undertaking which is full of disappointments. For though the service of others is a dream we like to indulge as the duty of our life, it is apt to be shattered by contact with individuals. And here endurance and longsuffering appear to be inseparably linked, for while endurance is related to life's circumstances, it is also brought into play by the offences of others for which the spirit of self-restraint, suspension of judgement and the temper of reconciliation are needed. There are some occasions of supreme difficulty arising from our contact with natures which we seem powerless to move to noble issues. Their faults seem ineradicable and their nemesis inevitable. Take the obvious example of Judas. In the end he proved his own worst enemy. He went his own way and finally to 'his own place.' But the love of his Master never failed under the strain to which it was subjected, though He suffered the anguish of watching the slow but inevitable issue of an evil purpose as it worked itself out to a doom which His love was powerless to avert. On the cross the divine prayer 'Father forgive them for they know not what they do' was the expression of his yearning compassion for souls which have gone astray through an overmastering perversity of will.

In fact, the test of Christian endurance lies frequently in the effort to escape from the grip of a personal prejudice, a grudge, a preconceived and often unjust impression which affects our attitude towards an individual and the cause he represents. Sooner or later we shall regret that endurance failed in its perfect work. It may have given out too soon and we have missed another of a Christian's opportunities to steer right onward in the pursuit of the prize of love.

Browning's phrases, 'the unlit lamp' and 'the ungirt loin,' remind us of the temptation which often assails us to give up a task laid upon us because of unconquered indolence or self-distrust, and thus to use Milton's great words, 'we slink out of the race where that immortal garland has to be run for, not without dust and heat.' We need not covet Henley's rather blatant and defiant attitude to life in reference to the setbacks and disappointments which sometimes leave us dispirited and broken-hearted. He speaks of his head as 'bloody but unbowed,' but let us desire rather the will of a Jacob wrestling with an unseen antagonist in desperation but with the resolve not to let him go without being blessed by him. To look the facts in the face and not be daunted by them is a first step to endurance.

St. Paul spoke of a 'crown of righteousness' as laid up for himself and all who loved the Lord's epiphany or manifestation. It is ours when we do not evade a plain duty or responsibility, as Jonah did, partly from lack of conviction, and partly because of what Stevenson's *Master of Ballantrae* called 'the malady of not wanting.' The crown or the immortal garland is not placed on our head by circumstances or by the esteem or goodwill of others. We win it for ourselves. No doubt a good name brings its own reward, but often merit languishes in obscurity. The real crown is the inward joy of knowing that we are approved by God, the testimony of a good conscience, of having merited the 'Well done!' of the Master of life.

St. Paul himself felt he was nothing if Christ was not magnified. If the fruit of his toil is longer to continue in the service of Christ he will dedicate the rest of his days to that service. He did not count himself to have attained, but he was not haunted, as so many souls are, by the tragedy of unfulfilment. He did endure. That was what one of the earliest of the apostolic fathers, Clement of Rome (1 Cor. v. 5), remarked as a note of his life: he had to meet rivalry and strife, but the experience enabled him to set forth 'the prize of endurance.' If he spoke of 'the love of God' as the object of a Christian's life, he linked with it as cause and effect 'the endurance of Christ' (2 Thess. iii. 5). So true is it that 'love endureth all things.'

Finally, St. Paul contructs a sort of ladder of Christian progress (Rom. v. 4). The lowest rung is tribulation, from which we rise to endurance. But the ascent still goes on; 'Blessed is the man who endureth trial,' says St. James (i. 12), here reminding us of a coincidence of thought and language which more than once reveals a certain community of spiritual wisdom between the two minds: for 'when he hath been approved' . . . St. Paul states this stage definitely. 'Endurance worketh experience,' that is, the man's character is approved as having revealed its steadfastness under trial. The final stage is hope. We end on the definitely Christian attitude to the sufferings of this life. They beget not pessimism but the sense of a larger destiny yet to be attained. It is no empty dream, for as the apostle adds, it does not disappoint: it is a hope that never puts us to shame, and of this the evidence is to be found in God's love, which is poured out in a continuous stream over us, so that in the great moods of inward exaltation

> Our souls have sight of that immortal sea
> Which brought us hither,
> Can in a moment travel thither,
> And see the Children sport upon the shore,
> And hear the mighty waters rolling ever more.

## CHAPTER XIII

## THE PERPETUAL OPPORTUNITY

WHEN the Apostle urges Timothy to 'be instant in season, out of season' (*eukairōs akairōs*, 2 Tim. iv. 2), he uses a striking and picturesque phrase intended to cover all situations and contingencies of life. To be 'in season' is evidently to be in the midst of such circumstances that an opportunity for holy service stares us in the face; no evasion of our duty is possible. On the other hand, to be 'out of season' suggests an occasion or environment where there is no favourable or even apparent opportunity for the exercise of our spiritual gifts. All the same, there *is* an opportunity; for whether *in season* or *out of season*, says the Apostle, we have to be instant. In the Christian calling *the opportunity is always with us*. The wise man said, 'To everything there is a season, and a time to every purpose under heaven.' And that is a doctrine which many a man of the world, many a man of action in politics and commerce, has echoed ever since. You are told to adapt your conduct to circumstances. Choose the right time for action. There are occasions when resolute action is a plain duty; there are others when it would be perilous to your interests. Your policy is to be determined by circumstances. But the Apostle suggests another

## The Perpetual Opportunity 103

course of action in the spiritual life. He teaches us that we may carry this spirit of opportunism or diplomacy too far. During the intervals when no 'opportunity' occurs, when we are in suspense, waiting for that tide in the affairs of men which is to be taken at the flood, our usefulness may be repressed when it should be exercised. We are such poor judges of what constitutes an 'opportunity,' that our safety lies in perceiving that every moment is an opportunity for service of some kind. Too often we do not detect the opportunity until it has vanished for ever, or we hesitate and are lost. Timothy, then, has not to be too diplomatic in his ministrations. He is not to regulate his enthusiasm by his surroundings. He is not to divide up his work into intervals of earnestness and inertia. He is neither to be intoxicated by success nor paralysed by failure. He is to do his work with a certain daring or 'dash,' in scorn of consequences; and he is to let his faith triumph over all obstacles, whether in his own emotions or in his outward surroundings.

This is a view of the religious life of which we need occasionally to be reminded; for *we are apt to make our service depend too exclusively on circumstances.* Most of us have been saddened by memories of failure in character, in will, in earnestness, and we trace our failure directly to subjection to our surroundings. It is natural for us to be at our best when we are in the atmosphere of sympathy, when those near us enter into our thoughts and ideals, when there is no discordant element of cynicism or hostility about us. We find that we are good when it is easy to be good, but our standard insensibly lowers when goodness requires a sacrifice. Like delicate plants, our virtues too quickly succumb to a change of temperature. If we are sincere with ourselves, we are little better than those whose religious emotions are stirred by their solitary act of Sabbath worship in the house of God, and then for the rest of the week sink into dull quiescence. We fall off in zeal when business engrosses, when a change of scene occurs, when success smiles upon us. Doubtless, it is a matter for rejoicing that there are few souls so dead that they do not respond to the solemnizing influence of a church, or a prayer, or some sacred association; yet it humiliates us to realize that our faith droops amid the common surroundings of life and has to be vitalized by special influences. If religion is to be more than the occasional stir of holy desire and thought, if it is to be the formative fact of conduct and life, we cannot be content with being instant only in season. But, also, when out of season, when the sacred influences are withdrawn and we pass from the mount of vision to the noisy street, we must have ears to hear the call of God, and we must be moved by the potent afflatus of His holy presence. The real musician will not do his best merely before the eager crowd of connoisseurs; but he will be true to his art—he will not be untrue to himself—if his listeners are hopelessly inartistic and ignorant.

## The Perpetual Opportunity

Thus our religious earnestness is worth little if it cannot stand the test of unhelpful circumstances. And yet how often it has been dwarfed by sorrow and adversity, been parched by the fret and fever of life, been blighted by the unkindly tempers and disappointing frowardness of those nearest us! And even in the sunshine of prosperity our high aims have dwindled away. For this hardening of our heart we are apt to lay the blame on circumstances. But is not the Christ within us to subdue all things to Himself? Is not the holy energy, imparted to us from above intended not only to carry us triumphantly through the common strife of life, but to gather force in the experience of striving? The light within the soul of a Christian is to reveal itself by changing earth to heaven, by sending shafts of radiance across the grey sea, by penetrating the dark corners of the world. Faith is not to be the victim of environment, but its conqueror.

There is, likewise, *a tyranny of moods as well as of circumstances*. In the energy of a revival, in the swing of sudden enthusiasm, the life of a church moves brightly, but it is apt to languish under the ordinary routine of worship and service. Depression—that common foe of the soul in modern life—is the mood that so often diminishes our zest for service. Forgetting that religion is God's message of joy—a joy unspeakable and full of glory—we fall away from God under the very trials which should remind us most of His nearness. Whether our low spirits be the result of physical weakness, or be a form of spiritual morbidness, *depression* is the signal not for sloth, not for languor in prayer and service, but rather for renewed activity. When the mist gathers about the liner in mid-ocean and the foghorn booms across the muffled air, all is energy and alertness; the crisis brings every nerve into play, and the seamen in charge are possessed by a grim, earnest sense of responsibility. So, when we are bewildered by doubt and cannot see far ahead, and our daily life becomes difficult and we are heavy laden, let us take as our motto the psalmist's words, ' My soul, wait thou only upon God,' and soon we shall say, ' We went through fire and water, but Thou broughtest us out into a wealthy place.'

There is also the mood of *weariness* which overtakes us in performing familiar duties. The very forms and phraseology of the religious life pall upon us. The glory of the first passion for God fades into the light of common day; and we behold like the blasé, world-wearied sage of old, ' nothing new under the sun.' We are disappointed with the seeming fruitlessness of our efforts to be good. The sense of our uselessness makes us tired of our task. *To be weary in well-doing*—who does not know that mood? When we find no joy in the sacred realities, the holy exercises, the great truths which filled us once with enthusiasm and buoyancy, then the labours of Christian service lose their interest. The outward task depends upon the inward vision. If the vision

## The Perpetual Opportunity 107

is clouded, the task is depreciated. Sometimes in the church as well as in the individual, this is a reaction from overstrained spiritual emotions, following on some spasmodic outburst of religious fervour. Now the *mood of enthusiasm and the mood of weariness alike test the sincerity of our religion.* We may, indeed, distrust ourselves if we only see the opportunities of holy service when our emotions are quickened by some artificial religious stimulant. And when we weary in well-doing, and see no opportunity left to us for the service of our fellows, it will be well for us to ask if we love God with all our heart, and with all our soul, and with all our strength, and with all our mind. We make too little of the will in our analysis of Christian experience. It is a will strengthened by constant communion with God that bears down the temptations arising from our changing and fickle dispositions—a will to do God's will at all costs. There is a self-surrender to Christ which is not the work of a moment, but of a life-time. Self-surrender is deepened within us as we emerge victoriously from each new struggle with our fickle moods and our baser selves. To be instant in season and out of season is to reject the leading of our temporary emotions, and to be guided by the will of Christ into loyal, true, steadfast service.

Finally, *we are inclined to place our opportunities in the future.* The future is to many of us the great opportunity for pleasing God. We are too ready to rest on what is going to be. We make our gifts, our self-sacrifice, and much of our service conditional on certain events happening in the future—increase of leisure, prosperity, an assured position, and even the meditative repose of old age. We catch ourselves constantly in the habit of shelving duties till a more convenient season—though the present moment may be a loud call to action. The future is for many of us the occasion for being instant and the climax of all our endeavours. Hence the idea that man can afford to live without religion till just on the threshold of eternity. The youth in his exuberance and *joie de vivre* says, 'Religion is for the days of manhood.' The man in the whirl of his restless ambitions and pursuits says, 'Religion is for the silence of old age.' The aged, looking back on his worldly life with a pang of remorse, says, 'Why did I not remember my Creator in the days of my youth?' It is against this postponement of energy that the Apostle warns his disciples. We have not to indulge in the habit of selecting opportunities, or marking out part of our uncertain life for what is claimed from us now. To put off into the future the duty of the moment—the decision which makes and re-makes character—is to weaken our power for holy, unselfish service. In the spiritual world the postponement of an opportunity, the evasion of the divine call, is fatal to all beauty and force of character; its nemesis is weakness of will, incompetence, and moral paralysis.

Thus, then, every moment is to be regarded by the Christian as an opportunity for the highest service;

and though the moments as they pass demand *different* service, they all demand *some* service. The command to be instant in season and out of season does not denote the ill-regulated or indiscreet zeal that uses religious phraseology on all occasions suitable and unsuitable; but it does mean that even when our lips are closed, there shall be no 'idle silence'; we shall really confess God, and our whole attitude and behaviour shall express our devotion to Him. It means, also, that when we are not doing definitely 'religious' work, when our task is what we call 'secular,' it shall be performed in a religious spirit. Sometimes it is the service of patience, quiet submission, of peacefulness, of earnest thought rather than of earnest action, that is demanded of us. The sentinel may be 'instant,' though his work in the darkness is but to watch and wait—as 'instant' indeed as the soldier in the thick of the fight. 'We[1] must work the works of Him that sent Me while it is day.' While life and power and thought are with us, while the light of life is ours—that light which is being stolen by the encroaching darkness—we must work, we must be instant, we must serve, so that when we come to 'the low dark verge of life,' and enter 'the twilight of eternal day,' we may be found in Him.

[1] See Revised Version of John ix. 4, the truth applying to disciples as well as to the Master.

## CHAPTER XIV

## THE HEAVENLY PLACES

READERS of the Pauline Epistles have, doubtless, noticed that the Apostle not infrequently sums up the argument or the standpoint of a given Epistle in one outstanding term or phrase. Such is the 'righteousness of God' of Romans, the 'faith in Christ' of Galatians, the 'fulness' (*plerōma*) of Colossians, the 'sound teaching' of 1 Timothy, and 'the heavenly places' of Ephesians.

Without discussing the question of the authenticity of the last-named Epistle, whether (in other words) it is Pauline or the work of a Paulinist, it is sufficient for our present purpose to point out that the occurrence of the unusual expression, 'the heavenly places,' (*ta epourania*) supports rather than otherwise the traditional view. Not only does the phrase appear five times in the Epistle; but it is so remarkable in itself, and so characteristic of this particular writing, that it is hardly likely to have been employed by one who sought to disguise his identity under a general resemblance to St. Paul's style and thought. The word does not occur in the Greek Old Testament, except as an epithet of God in two passages in 3 Macc. So far as Hellenistic Greek is concerned, it is a distinctively New Testament epithet; but it is also

## The Heavenly Places

found in Homer and Plato, and therefore is evidently drawn from the classical Hellenic stock.[1] While the epithet 'heavenly' is found elsewhere (four times) in the Pauline Epistles, it is the use of the phrase in Ephesians which concerns us now.

It is clear that 'the heavenly places' is equivalent to 'the unseen world' or 'the unseen,' which might fitly be regarded as an attempted rendering. It is not to be regarded as a mere synonym of heaven, if by heaven we mean a future state of being. For St. Paul it eternally exists; it is a sphere outside of time, a spiritual universe: a vast realm of the noumenal behind the world of sense. By its use, 'St. Paul warns us,' says Armitage Robinson, 'that he takes the suprasensual view of life.'

The following are the salient points of the five passages referred to: i. 3; i. 20; ii. 6; iii. 10; vi. 12. Taking the last two passages together as introducing us to the conceptions of Jewish angelology, we discover that in the Apostle's mind the unseen world was peopled by spirits both good and evil. While in the Epistle to the Colossians he speaks with impatience of the elaborate orders of the celestial hierarchy as conceived by Gnostic Judaizers, here and elsewhere the Apostle reveals no divergence from the current Jewish views of the spiritual world.

[1] Nageli (*Der Wortschatz des apostels Paulus*) notes its occurrence in 2 Tim. iv. 18, but does not include it in his list of Ionic-poetic Pauline words, where it may fitly find a place. It is found in the great Paris magical papyrus, which shows it had survived in Hellenistic Greek outside the New Testament, Moulton and Milligan, *Vocabulary of the Greek Testament*, s.v.

When he regards the heavenly sphere as the habitation of hostile powers arrayed against the Christian warrior, we are immediately reminded of the speculations of the Jewish apocalypses. The supra-terrestrial region is the counterpart of a visible world, where good and evil are in perpetual conflict. 'The prince of the power of the air' (ii. 2), with his legions that 'rule this dark world' (vi. 12), occupies the unseen world, and carries on his operations there—a defeated and inferior,[1] although malignant, being. The conclusion which the Apostle draws from this remarkable conception of the heavenly sphere as the scene of a spiritual warfare is the practical injunction: 'Put on the whole armour of God.' The warfare is spiritual, therefore the weapons must be spiritual.

On the other hand, there is a hierarchy of good spirits in the unseen; and it is evidently of these that the Apostle thinks when he utters his glowing words regarding the function of the Church. The community of Christians who are saved by faith in Christ exist to set forth 'to the principalities and powers in the heavenly places the variegated wisdom of God.' 'Ecclesia,' says Calvin, 'quasi speculum in quo contemplantur angeli mirificam Dei sapientiam quam prius nescierant.' Yet we cannot but believe that the apostolic vision also included, even in this

---

[1] cf. Edwards (on 1 Cor. v. 5), dealing with the Jewish conception of Satan. 'The correct view seems to be that Christ and His Apostles combined the Zoroastrian doctrine of an antagonist of God with the early Hebrew doctrine of Satan's inferiority to God (cf. Isa. xlv. 18).'

connexion, the forces of the unseen which were opposed to the Divine will. The good and evil Potencies of the heavenly sphere are regarded as spectators of the Church, which is to enlighten their ignorance of the Divine purpose—a purpose which was formed before the creation, in that it centred in the eternal Christ.

It is clear from the tenor of these passages, especially when taken along with the phrase already quoted from ii. 2, 'the prince of the power of the air,' that St. Paul's view of the heavenly places is not wholly liberated from the sense of space and locality, which colours Jewish angelology. Lightfoot[1] has pointed out that 'things in the heaven' are not quite equivalent to 'things unseen' in Pauline language. 'Heaven and earth together comprehend all space; and all things, whether material or immaterial, are conceived . . . as having their abode in space.'

But in considering the other three passages, we leave behind us Jewish ideas and pass into a Hellenic order of thought. The unseen world of St. Paul is focussed in Christ. He no longer knows Christ 'after the flesh'; that is, Christ is no longer to be apprehended through the forms of sense-perception: He is a spiritual Person. Hence the conception of the exalted Christ lifts St. Paul into the noumenal world; to use his own phrase, Christ makes him to sit, together with all the saints, 'in the heavenly places' (ii. 6). 'The heavenly places' are the home

[1] See note on Col. i. 6.

of the exalted, spiritual Christ (i. 20). The saint who is 'in Christ' shares His life, and therefore has access to His home. He is therefore fitly described as blest 'with all spiritual blessing' (i. 3).

Such is the language of one who views all things *sub specie aeternitatis* and to whom 'the super-sensible has the reality of the sensible.' If sometimes St. Paul's diction recalls Aristotle, it more frequently reminds us of Plato. That the Jewish world was subtly interpenetrated by the influences of Greek philosophy, we can no longer doubt. If we wish to realize how the mind of a Jew could absorb Greek philosophy and become for its age the mind of a new theologian, we have but to turn to Philo, with whose writings the Apostle was well acquainted, if the judgement of competent scholars may be accepted. Readers of Kingsley's *Hypatia* will remember with what cogency Raphael Aben-Ezra expounded the Platonic origin of St. Paul's doctrine of the archetypal Man. James Adam, in his *Religious Teachers of Greece,* points out the affinities of Plato's psychology and St. Paul's. Lightfoot and Ramsay agree in the conviction that the influence of Stoicism is very marked upon the diction and the doctrine of the Apostle : and we cannot doubt that the teachings of the Academy were equally familiar to him. For both St. Paul and Plato 'the visible is an image of the invisible.' It is at least conceivable that but for the Platonic theory of ideas St. Paul's conception of the spiritual Christ would not have been framed in the

## The Heavenly Places

terms which are familiar to us in his Epistles, especially those to the Colossians and Ephesians, while the Platonism of his thought may have inspired the argument of the author of the Epistle to the Hebrews and the prologue of the Fourth Gospel.

At the same time, St. Paul by his identification of the historical Jesus with the spiritual Christ escaped the abstractness which attaches to Plato's presentation of the ideas and avoided the superfluous dualism of the sensible particular and its spiritual counterpart, to which Aristotle, not without reason, objected in his criticism of the Platonic theory. The Christ of the heavenly places is not a logical abstraction: He is one with the crucified Jesus. Thus St. Paul's mystical conception of the unseen is never divorced from reality. To be *in Christ* is not a vague aspiration, but a practical experience. Christ does not, like the Platonic idea, transcend existence: He bridges in Himself the chasm between earth and heaven, the seen and the unseen.

Thus, while St. Paul's language in his case of the phrase ' the heavenly places ' suggests mysticism, his mystical conception of the unseen as the spiritual background of human life is always *practical*. It is never a mere nebulous idealism that stands out of relation to the common experiences of life, its changes, its sorrows, its daily frictions and disappointments, its rises and its falls. In the midst of all, St. Paul

> by the vision splendid
> Is on his way attended.

Thus the Divine wisdom would seem to have used Plato[1] as a preparer of His way and Platonic thought as a foregleam of 'a better hope'—the conception of the unseen as the Home of the Ideal Christ, the Spiritual Head of the Church. We owe not a little to such writers as the Cambridge Platonists for expounding from the standpoint occupied by St. Paul a similar view of religion as spiritualizing material things.

Listen, for example, to John Smith in his famous sermon on *The Excellency and Nobleness of True Religion*. 'True religion never finds itself out of the infinite sphere of the Divinity, and wherever it finds beauty, harmony, goodness, love, ingenuousness, wisdom, holiness, justice, and the like, it is ready to say, Here, and there is God: wheresoever any such perfections shine out, a holy mind climbs up by these sunbeams, and raises itself to God.' Or we may turn for an even more striking conception of the powers of the soul to a passage in the works of the greatest Christian Platonist among English poets, William Wordsworth. It occurred to the writer's mind on a certain occasion in the Lake district when he witnessed a scene not unlike that described in the quotation. In the foreground a group of dusky firs and evergreens; beneath the overhanging boughs the gleam of the lake of Bassenthwaite; in the background the mysterious dim outline of Skiddaw 'and the moon was full.'

[1] cf. Justin, Apol. ii. 13.

## The Heavenly Places

> Within the soul a faculty abides
> That with interpositions, which would hide
> And darken, so can deal that they become
> Contingencies of pomp; and serve to exalt
> Her native brightness. As the ample moon,
> In the deep stillness of a summer even
> Rising behind a thick and lofty grove,
> Burns, like an unconsuming fire of light,
> In the green trees: and, kindling on all sides
> Their leafy umbrage, turns the dusky veil
> Into a substance glorious as her own,
> Yea, with her own incorporated, by power
> Capacious and serene. Like power abides
> In man's celestial spirit: virtue thus
> Sets forth and magnifies herself; thus feeds
> A calm, a beautiful, and silent fire,
> From the encumbrances of mortal life,
> From error, disappointment—nay, from guilt;
> And sometimes, so relenting justice wills,
> From palpable oppressions of despair.[1]

No image could more fitly express the transforming power exercised upon the experiences of life by the abiding sense of the unseen. Gleams of 'the heavenly places' lit up for St. Paul the darkest disciplines of the soul, and he could face without despair 'the sufferings of this present time,' because he was able in the power of His Master ever to discern through time's many-coloured dome 'the white radiance of eternity.'

[1] *Excursion*, iv. 1055-1077.

## CHAPTER XV

## CONTENTMENT

*I have learned, in whatsoever state I am, therein to be content* (Phil. iv. 11, R.V.).

IF we may venture to substitute for the familiar rendering 'content' the expression 'self-sufficing,' we get more speedily to the heart of the original word (*autarkēs*). For what St. Paul has learned is not so much to be contented with the circumstances of his life as to be altogether independent of them. He means something deeper and more spiritual than that sense of placid satisfaction with one's environment and possibly with oneself which the word 'contentment' is popularly supposed to convey. Nor does he refer to the philosophic calm of the Stoic. He certainly uses a Stoic word; but St. Paul was no Stoic. He believed that 'to them that love God all things work together for good.' The God of the Stoics was in no sense personal. He was identified with nature. Consequently the circumstances of the individual life were products of an unalterable law. The only way to meet fate was to cultivate an unconquerable soul. Self-sufficingness meant hard, proud, passive indifference to events which man was powerless either to order or to change. It is easy to see that Stoicism is an impossible gospel for average human nature. Who, without reliance on a higher Will, can really come to regard pain, loss, and disease as if they were not? Who, apart from a divine strength, is so strong that the impact of sorrows leaves no furrow on his face, no wound in his soul? To whom can fatalism bring calm, except 'a calm despair'? The Stoic was the creature of a loveless creed; he reached a certain independence of soul, but in saving himself he lost sight of others; sympathy died out of him.

What then was the secret and the character of St. Paul's self-sufficingness? His was no easy life; indeed all the elements that make for 'contentment' were absent. He was lonely, uncheered by joys and companionships of home, conscious of his physical uncomeliness, suffering from a painful disease, scoffed at by the Greeks for his unintelligible speculations, distrusted by his own nation for his too catholic sympathies. The cares of a mighty parish lay on his soul. The charge of hundreds of half-tutored souls, just emerging from the darkness of heathendom, was in his keeping,

> Desperate tides of the whole great world's anguish
> Forced through the channels of a single heart.

He knew the depressions of hopeless failure; he knew what it was to be distrusted by his own, and also, what is worse, to distrust his own; he was wounded in the house of his friends. But no hero was ever more sunny, more hopeful than he. Cheerfully, steadily he went about the mission of his life. His soul never hardened; his joy never grew dim; the springlike purity of his quiet spirit was never blighted. How was he self-sufficing? Simply because he had *within* himself resources compared with which the *outward* elements of life were as naught. His true wealth lay in the storehouse of his soul. The accidents of existence beat in vain against the doors of that spiritual treasury. Christ was in him, the hope of glory. The secret attacks of depression and temptation failed against a citadel of which the peace of Christ was the trusty sentinel. The sentiment of a poet like Shelley in the lines,

> I could lie down like a tired child,
> And weep away the life of care
> Which I have borne and yet must bear,

will find no echo in a deeply spiritual nature. St. Paul would reply, 'In all these things we are more than conquerors.' The poet's whole career was the history of one overcome; it was the confession of defeat. When St. Paul was pierced by the thorn in the flesh, the Spirit of God stilled rebellion into peace. He was self-sufficing because he believed so entirely the message of the divine voice, 'My grace is sufficient for thee.' He gloried in infirmities that the power of Christ might overshadow him; under that sheltering tent he was safe.

Another influence that made for self-sufficingness was his belief that his life was being shaped by a divine Artificer, through divers processes, into the image of the heavenly. He could 'welcome each rebuff that turned earth's smoothness rough'; for the Potter was moulding the cup into something rich and strange. 'The marks of the Lord Jesus'—the furrows of care, the scars of persecution—were evidences that God was engaged in the making of his soul. His true compensation for life's limitations lay in the consciousness that a divine Will was educating him for the world of light. Says George Eliot: 'In the time when sorrow has become stale, and has no longer an emotive intensity that counteracts the pain—in the time when day follows day in dull, unexpectant sameness, and trial is a dreary routine—it is then that despair threatens; it is then that the peremptory hunger of the soul is felt, and eye and ear are strained after some unlearned secret which shall give to endurance the nature of satisfaction.' But St. Paul had grasped this secret; for does he not say, 'Everywhere and in all things have I been instructed in the mystic secret both to be full and to be hungry, both to abound and to suffer need'? For the lowliest believer in Christ 'the peremptory hunger of the soul' is for ever satisfied. 'By what,' asks Amiel, 'has Christianity subdued the world if not by the apotheosis of grief, by its marvellous transmutation of suffering into triumph, of the crown of thorns into the crown of triumph?' He that has been crucified with Christ finds suffering to be 'a strange initiation into happiness.'

The external aspect of life, for thousands of our

fellow creatures, may indeed depress us to-day. We become dumb in the grey monotony of a great industrial city or mining centre. We think of the strength which is spent for that which satisfieth not in the whir of the factory, in the dull routine of trade, in the gloom of the deep-hidden mine. But the outward sphere is not all. For many a lowly, trustful heart there is an inner career of peace and joy, a secret world of holy thought, of celestial aspiration. Within the sheltering walls of the spirit is a garden radiant with the flowers of eternity and watered by the ministry of unsleeping Love. We can never measure a Christian's horizon by what we call his 'secular' life; his citizenship is in heaven; 'at noonday in the bustle of man's worktime, he greets the unseen with a cheer.'

It is a commonplace perhaps to insist that in the average Christian we miss this fruitage of self-sufficingness. It may be that the materialism of the age is partly responsible for this. Many in their eager pursuit of the *outward* resources that go as they think to the making of life, lose sight of the *inner*. They have come to regard religion as settling for them the character of their future in the next stage of being; but it does not by itself supply the deficiencies of the life that now is. They exalt possessions above character, a living above a life. Now, growth in grace means an enlargement of our estimate of the spiritual. When we develop in the knowledge of Christ, we learn on what elements of our earthly existence to lay the emphasis. 'He that is spiritual judgeth all things.' His standard of valuation rises. He discriminates between the real and the fleeting, the true and the false. The Apostle's definition of life was compact and final: to live is Christ. It is easy to fritter away our spiritual gifts and energies in a fruitless ambition to reach a sphere which we were never intended to fill, instead of using those gifts and energies in an endeavour to adorn nobly and wisely the sphere in which we have been placed. It is right to covet earnestly the best gifts; but the best gifts are often reached by those who are content to fill a little space. The worst way in which to qualify for a higher position is to despise the opportunities of the present one. When we are seized with a feverish craving for a new series of sensations, when old duties pall, when we weary of the task imposed on us, when the spirit is torn by restlessness, we need to ask ourselves whether we have really seen Christ and learnt St. Paul's lesson.

It is significant that the Apostle learnt his lesson of self-sufficingness all at once ('I learnt,' not 'I have learned,'[1] as the student will remark). It did not come to him solely through the patient discipline of years; it flashed upon him in the great moment of his history. When he knew the power of Christ's resurrection, the true explanation of life dawned on him; the world suddenly wore a new expression.

[1] The English idiom, however, requires this translation of the original aorist tense.

> World—how it walled about
>   Life with disgrace,
> Till God's own smile came out;
>   That was thy face.

His personal union with Christ was the secret of his spiritual independence. His was the noble self-sufficiency which consists in the merging of one's self in Christ; consequently it meant, not the loss of sympathy, but the deepening of sympathy with others. The Stoic's self-sufficiency was self-absorption, self-isolation; St. Paul, linked with Christ, abiding in Christ, appropriated ever more deeply his Master's patient love. It is only by being imitators of St. Paul that we shall come to see, as he saw, a different meaning in the limitations of earthly life; and it is only thus that we shall lose that fretfulness which wears down the soul and dims the vision of Christ. The conclusion of the whole matter may be given in the eloquent lines of F. W. H. Myers, which state St. Paul's spiritual creed:

> Yea, thro' life, death, thro' sorrow and thro' sinning,
>   He shall suffice me, for He hath sufficed;
> Christ is the end, for Christ was the beginning;
>   Christ the beginning, for the end is Christ.

## CHAPTER XVI

## THE MIRROR AND THE RIDDLE

*Now we see in a mirror, darkly* (*Gr. : in a riddle*); *but then face to face* (1 Cor. xiii. 12, R.V. and *marg.*).

HERE is a thought that underlies all the Apostle's thinking. We are living in a world of symbols. All objects of our thought are but representations—pictures or reflections of unseen realities. What has been revealed is valid so far as it goes; but it has only the validity of a reflection in a mirror (*esoptron*). What is to be revealed hereafter is the perfect. What we behold to-day is the partial. We now see by means of a mirror. But revelation is not only a reflection; it bears the aspect of a riddle (*ainigma*), of which the ultimate solution is for the moment beyond us. We are for ever running into problems, brushing against the veil, the impenetrable veil of mystery; but the answer evades us. The riddle is propounded only to be given up.

It might appear that this is but the observation of the familiar fact that our faculties are those of finite beings; but the words bear upon the future rather than the present, and reach out with brave certainty from the incompleteness of time to a coming completeness, from the symbol to the reality, from vision to intuition. The theology of the Apostle is a theology of wide perspectives. Like an expanse of sea merging away into the golden sky of evening, such was life and revelation to his spirit. Both are sharply defined and bounded to the superficial mind; but to him their horizons bordered on infinity. He knew there were limits to our knowledge, but the limits were not final, only temporary. Our knowledge of God, of the world, of ourselves, brings us ever to the portals of mystery; but there is a Beyond where the hidden shall be revealed, where the reflection in the glass shall be superseded by a living face and the enigma by certainty. What do we know of God? We know Him only in reflection. Of Him we say with Hooker, ' Our soundest knowledge is to know that we know Him not, as indeed He is, neither can know Him '; or with Dr. Watts:

> Beneath Thy feet we lie afar
> And see but shadows of Thy face.

1. We see the divine life *in the mirror of nature*. ' For the invisible things of Him since the creation of the world are clearly seen, being perceived through the things that are made, even His everlasting power and divinity.' God is thus a necessity of thought. The beauty of the created universe runs back to a higher Beauty. Its orderly procession of life is the visible expression of a primal Life, itself underived. And the rhythmical movement of starry worlds is the reflection of an eternal order in the mind of the Deity. We find everywhere ' a Presence that disturbs us with the joy of elevated thoughts '—a spirit that

rolls through all things. It is no poetic fiction, but a true conception which is uttered by the Earth-spirit in Goethe's *Faust*:

> 'Tis thus at the roaring loom of time I ply
> And weave for God the garment thou see'st Him by.

The panorama of the universe is the mantle of the eternal—the vesture through which His glory shines. This is the underlying thought of *Sartor Resartus*; for Carlyle's hero 'pierced into the mystery of the world, recognizing in the highest sensible phenomena, so far as sense went, only fresh or faded raiment; yet ever under this a celestial essence thereby rendered visible.' We do not walk in a dead world which the Deity has left to itself, to the operation of its own machine-like laws; but in one that thrills and throbs with His presence. The understanding heart, the seeing eye, finds Him everywhere. We trace Him in every stream and hill. The woods break out into singing before Him, and the forests clap their hands. The heavens declare His glory. The firmament showeth His handiwork. The joy of the world is the utterance of His own rapture; and its symmetry and excellence the mirror of His wisdom.

2. We see God also *in the mirror of the Incarnate Word*. To St. Paul God is the Father of our Lord Jesus Christ, and Jesus Christ is the manifestation of God in time. The Christ of the Gospels is the eternal and the divine enshrined in a human life. 'That which was from the beginning' is also 'that which we have seen with our eyes, that which we

beheld and our hands handled.' The mind of Christ is a transcript of God's. We read in His teaching and in His character, His gentleness and graciousness, His sense of the dignity of man as man, and His forgiving love, a presentation of the Father's inner life. He gathers into Himself the rays of the One Light, He is the effulgence of the Father's glory. It is not that God assumed a human form as a temporary guise, which was no new thought, at least to classical theology; it was God taking up humanity into Himself, and thereby carrying out into the processes of time an eternal relationship. For 'the firstborn of all creation' revealed in Himself the essential union between God and man. Therefore if we have eyes to see, we may behold in Christ, as in a mirror, at once the perfection of Humanity and the glory of God. He represents the highest to which man could rise, the lowest to which God could stoop. To many of His own contemporaries His real nature was as a sealed book, and to very many since He passed from the earth He has appeared but a man—an image of nothing greater than Himself, except in the sense that He too, like all men, is the off-spring of God. But there were those, like St. Peter and St. John, who came to understand that they had been gazing at God as in a mirror, and saw in their Master the very Son of the Eternal; and there was Thomas, bound so long to outward things, who pierced at length to the inner suprasensible meaning of the Risen One, and exclaimed: 'My Lord and my God!' Thus, those who saw our Lord in the days of His flesh did not at once rise to the full knowledge of what He was. And we of to-day who know Him not only from the portrait of the Gospels, but from His appeal to our conscience—how slow are we to recognize in His coming, His cross, and His resurrection the symbols in time of eternal truths! Take His coming—what was it if not the earthly sign that God is ever lifting up man to His heart and to His life? And the cross— is it not the symbol of God's eternal sorrow over human disobedience and His passion to redeem? And the resurrection of our Lord is the revelation to the eye of faith of a life that knows no ending, and of the fact that with God there is no death. We behold this wonderful human life, beginning in the lowly manger of Bethlehem, passing almost at once into the 'sanctuary of sorrow,' yielding itself at length in love to the death of the cross, and thence emerging into the glorified life of God; and the sufficient explanation thereof is that we have before us the purposes and thoughts, the passion and the love of Deity. On the wider plane it presents the same truth which is shadowed forth in the feast ordained by our Lord, where the visible symbols of bread and wine have a spiritual significance, in that through and beyond them we reach out to the very life of our souls—to the visible Christ upon whom in our spirit we feed. Thus, the revelation of God in Christ is a sacrament, is a visible reflection of that which through endless ages has been hidden from us.

3. We also behold God *mirrored in man, in ourselves*. He has left not Himself without witness in our consciousness. We find Him within us. Man cannot get away from God: 'it is because there is an infinite in him which, with all his cunning, he cannot quite bury under the finite.' There is that within man which is not part of the visible universe; that which indeed is the condition of there being a visible universe. How can we be conscious of nature if there is not within us a faculty not itself of nature, which makes nature? There is a true supernatural within us which is the condition of all knowledge, and which enables us to say 'I am,' and 'I am not,' and thus to realize our distinct personality and freedom. This takes us back to an eternal consciousness. 'God created man in His own image.' In our conscience, in our will, in the depths of our spirit, we behold as in a mirror the infinite being—the God in whose nature we bear a part. The human personality, with its pitiful sense of finitude and imperfection, presupposes the ultimate personal life of Deity. Our hope of becoming like God lies in the fact that we are like Him already, and that even now we share in His nature. The ascent of man to God is only possible because God is already attained by man.

Yet when we have said this and vindicated in some measure the sufficiency and validity of God's self-revelation, we cannot but admit that it is only an arc of a perfect whole. We have the mirror—the valid and true reflection of God. But the riddle is also with us—the haunting sense of an enigma beyond our clearest apprehension—of a knowledge relatively to our condition ample and complete, yet in itself a fragment of an infinite world. Much is revealed; who can say how much is hidden? Nowhere can we find a more beautiful expression of this thought than in Wordsworth's lines on the shell in which a curious child ' dwelling upon a tract of inland ground ' hears the murmurs of the distant ocean:

> Even such a shell the universe itself
> Is to the ear of Faith, and there are times,
> I doubt not, when to you it doth impart
> Authentic tidings of invisible things:
> Of ebb and flow and ever-during power,
> And central peace, subsisting at the heart
> Of endless agitation.

True, we have received 'authentic tidings'; who can doubt it? But the enigma remains; the ocean of truth is beyond us untraversed and immeasurable. We hear its far-off rolling tides in the few shells we have gathered from its shores. Wherever we turn the riddle meets us. Whether it be to the consideration of evil, its beginning, its existence, its triumphs, or the explanation of human experience, of sorrow, of pain, of death, the why and the wherefore eludes us. We are to ourselves an enigma, and the wayside flower, like life, is a thing incomprehensible. Science in its onward march but deepens our sense of the mysterious, and the ultimate nature of a common fact like electricity baffles analysis.

Is it not well, however, to remember the fact that

we *see*? There is a vision, albeit dim, vouchsafed to faith; a vision of which the very imperfectness is the promise of a final and ineffable illumination.

'But then FACE TO FACE.'

The symbolical will become the immediate and the intuitive. To-day—as it has ever been—it is hard to get people to *see*. Their gaze is on the outward—the shows of sense and of time—upon the seen; and therefore to the New Testament writers it is but blindness. To them he who does not see the unseen, does not see at all. But, given the vision of faith, it will develop from faltering dim beginnings, and its horizons will become richer and more heavenly. It will rejoice in the mirror. It will not even resent the riddle. And why? Because it is conscious of moving onwards to the Face. The late Professor T. C. Edwards says that St. Paul got his metaphor of the mirror from Philo, who got it from Plato, and he mentions the striking passage in Plato's *Republic*,[1] where Socrates is illustrating the slow development of our faculties by the case of men immured in a cavern who are suddenly dragged into the sunlight. Not a man at first can make out, in the unaccustomed glare, a single object as it is. 'Hence, I suppose, habit will be necessary to enable him to perceive objects in that upper world. At first he will be most successful in distinguishing shadows; then he will discern the reflections of men and other things in water, and afterwards the realities; and after this he

[1] *Republic*, vii. 516 (trans. Davies & Vaughan).

will raise his eyes to encounter the light of the moon and the stars, finding it less difficult to study the heavenly bodies and the heaven itself by night than the sun and the sun's light by day.' Finally, he will see the sun as it *is,* not as it *appears* in water or on alien ground, and then he will conclude that the sun is the author of the seasons, the guardian of the visible world, and the cause of all he and his friends used to see. On some such lines the idealism of St. Paul runs respecting the soul and its spiritual vision as it ascends from the partial to the perfect, from the fleeting to the real. One may note, in passing, the joy of discovering a kinship between such minds as Plato, St. Paul, and Wordsworth, children of ages far distant, but each illumined by the immanent Reason, by ' the light that lighteth every man.'

Listen to John Smith, the Cambridge Platonist: ' We cannot here see *in speculo lucido :* here we can see *but in a glass,* and that *darkly* too. Our own *Imaginative* Powers, which are perpetually attending the highest acts of our Souls, will be breathing a grosse dew upon the pure glasse of our Understandings, and so sully and besmear it, that we cannot see the Image of the Divinity sincerely in it. But yet this knowledge being a true heavenly fire kindled from God's own Altar, begets an undaunted courage in the Souls of good men, and enables them to cast a holy Scorn upon the poor, petty trash of this Life in comparison with Divine things. . . . This Sight of God makes pious Souls breathe after that blessed time when Mortality shall be swallowed up of Life, when they shall no more behold the Divinity through those dark Mediums that eclipse the blessed Sight of it.'[1]

Now, that God dwells in a glory which is inaccessible, is not an argument for a restless, fretful spirit or for a sullen and defiant stoicism. It may be that life owes its richness to the meanings that elude us and the truths that have been half revealed and half concealed. It is surely right for us, constituted as we are, to desire with Lessing the search for truth rather than the gift of all truth itself. What is demanded of us in face of 'the unsolved mystery of things' is not the stagnation of listless indifference nor the angry resentment of a baffled intellect, but the calm repose of faith. How nobly this spirit of placid assurance pervades the apostolic writings! There is no mad beating of the wings against the cage. There is no melancholy; still less what we call pessimism. There is gratitude for what has been revealed. There is deep joy in the thought of what is yet to be revealed. 'Then,' says the Apostle, in an ecstasy of gladness, 'shall I know fully, even as also I have been known.' To him that is the conclusion of the whole matter. The mists will vanish. Already indeed they are interpenetrated with shafts of glory; and he will one day emerge into the light of the beatific Face.

[1] The conclusion of the sermon on 'The True Way or Method of Attaining Divine Knowledge.'

## CHAPTER XVII

## INDWELLING POWER

*Most gladly therefore will I rather glory in my weakness, that the power of Christ may rest upon me* (2 Cor. xii. 9).

It is not easy to discern the reason why St. Paul should use in this passage the very rare verb (*episkēnoō*) ' rest,' when other more familiar expressions might have even more clearly indicated his meaning. The lexicographers can quote no parallels in the whole range of Greek literature, except two passages in Polybius, where the word is used in a military connexion of soldiers lodging or being billeted in certain houses. There is no example in the Greek O.T. The Vulgate renders the verb by *inhabitet*. Bengel makes the word practically synonymous with ' overshadow,' which is used in Exod. xl. 35 as a translation of the Hebrew verb for the Shekinah abiding on the Tabernacle. The uncompounded verb, which is used in Rev. xii. 12, xiii. 6, xxi. 3, is found in John i. 14 in the greatest of all statements, ' The Word became flesh and *tabernacled* among us.'

The phrase ' the power of Christ ' is not so familiar to St. Paul's readers as ' the power of God,' or the power which is associated with the Spirit. But in verse 9 of this chapter power is evidently to be understood of the Lord's power; while in 1 Cor. v. 4, where the excommunication of the incestuous person is referred to, St. Paul expressly indicates that the spiritual authority of Christ Himself which is imparted to the Church, brings additional weight to that solemn decision. Undoubtedly the passage before us offers an obvious analogy to statements referring to the illapse or descent of the Divine Spirit; but St. Paul never explicitly refers to the historical event of Pentecost. He regarded the Spirit as the permanent possession of humanity and as 'the active principle of Christ's personality,' going indeed so far as to identify the Spirit with the Person of Christ, e.g. ' The Lord is the Spirit ' (2 Cor. iii. 17), and again, ' We are changed into the same image by the Lord, the Spirit ' (2 Cor. iii. 18). But such passages are to be regarded as indicating his profound conviction that ' it is only through our connexion with Christ's Person and our faith in Him that we experience that specific working of God's Spirit that was exemplified supremely in His life ' (Somerville's *St. Paul's Conception of Christ*, p. 120). Without in any way detracting from the work of the Divine Spirit, St. Paul frequently describes it in terms of the glorified Christ. Consequently the dynamic of Christ may be appropriately described as resting upon the individual in the same way as the Divine Spirit rests upon him.

By the aid of such data we can arrive at a fairly definite impression of the meaning of the Apostle's

## Indwelling Power

words in 2 Cor. xii. 9. The thorn in the flesh, whatever its nature, was regarded as a humbling, if painful, discipline. The pain was keen enough to move the Apostle to pray that it might be removed. The prayer was answered in the Lord's own way. 'My grace is sufficient for thee: for power (or my power) is made perfect in weakness.' When the Apostle realized this to be the ultimate purpose of the suffering, he not only accepted his infirmities but gloried in them. So far from resenting the discipline, he was prepared to make a boast of it, to the end that the power,[1] which was so to be perfected, might indeed rest upon him. The Revisers' marginal comment on the rendering 'rest upon me' is 'cover me, Gr. *spread a tabernacle over me*.' Bengel took the word in effect as equivalent to 'overshadow,' and, translating the passage *ut tanquam tentorium superobtegat me,* decides against the idea of 'inhabitation' as tending to impair the Apostle's sense of weakness. No doubt the conception of Christ's power as a sheltering tent is attractive (cp. p.120 *sup.*); but we agree with the Revisers in adopting a rendering which is more in harmony with the only extant examples of its usage and with the formation of the word itself, namely, to rest upon, encamp or settle upon, fix a tent or home in. True, a 'tent' is not a permanent dwelling-place, but to a nomadic people

---

[1] The R.V. reverses the translation of A.V., giving 'power' for *dynamis* in the earlier part of the verse, and 'strength' in the later; but there seems to be no adequate reason for the alteration in the rendering of the word either in the A.V. or R.V.

or to an army on campaign it was their home. Again, the word 'tent' is the Greek Old and New Testament word for the Tabernacle of Israel. The Tabernacle was not the Temple, but none the less it was the symbol of the permanent realization of God's Presence in Israel. Hence, while the concept of 'tent' or 'tabernacle' implies transitoriness, it also carries with it the further ideas of sanctity, communion, rest, protection. It is curious, indeed, when we remember that St. Paul was a weaver of tent cloth, that the word 'tent' so familiar in the Epistle to the Hebrews does not occur in Pauline language, though there is a similar form of the word (2 Cor. v. 4) when the body is spoken of as the tent or tabernacle of the soul. When St. Paul speaks of 'the power of Christ' (which may be interpreted 'Christ as Power') resting upon him, he has perhaps lost sight of the transiency associated with the word 'tent' and been influenced by the more august conception which the term would convey to the Hebrew mind. But apart from this, the word is in harmony with the fleetingness of human life; cf. the touching lament of Hezekiah, Isa. xxxviii. 12, 'Mine age ... is carried away from me as a shepherd's tent.' Certainly there is nothing out of place in the conception of Christ's Power making a kind of earthly home or shrine for itself in the heart of the saint. The enshrinement of a divine Power in human nature—this is the essence of the Christian revelation as well as the secret of a noble character.

The context suggests that such power comes as

the issue of suffering nobly borne and nobly understood. The latter for the purposes of life is as important as the former. Many a man who has no personal experience of religion can bear bodily infirmity without flinching or murmuring; but he has a secret resentment against the discipline of suffering and against the forces of the universe which seem to thrust it upon him. Now, St. Paul was not only a brave sufferer, but he was a brave interpreter of suffering. Over against weakness he placed power, and that power, spiritual; nay, the very power of Christ Himself which, lighting upon him, made his being its home. F. W. H. Myers is here one of our most helpful interpreters, thus rendering the Apostle's testimony to his Lord:

> He as he wills shall solder and shall sunder,
>   Slay in a day and quicken in an hour,
> Tune him a music from the Sons of Thunder,
>   Forge and transform my passion into power.
>
> Ay, for this Paul, a scorn and a despising,
>   Weak as you know him and the wretch you see,—
> Even in these eyes shall ye behold him rising,
>   Strength in infirmities and Christ in me.

Again, in another passage, where the same poet compares the sudden inspiration of the saint with the bursting into flame of a glorious pæan in the soul of an Ægean bard, the power of Christ becomes a wondrous and thrilling possession from above.

> Scarcely I catch the words of his revealing,
>   Hardly I hear him, dimly understand,
> Only the Power that is within me pealing
>   Lives on my lips and beckons to my hand.

The power of Christ comes, then, in response not only to courageous endurance, but to courageous acceptance of suffering. His Will is not only our Peace but our Power. One of the obvious marks of second-century Christianity, if we may judge by the testimony of contemporary writers, was the fact of a strange moral power which was at work in the Christian communities making the sinful pure, the selfish loving, the shrinking brave even to death and transforming thousands of quiet obscure people into saints and heroes. There was only one explanation. 'These things seem not to be the works of man: these things are the power of God,' said the author of the Epistle to Diognetus, that charming early defence of Christianity by an unknown author. And it has been so through the ages. Amid the sorrows and pains of the struggling souls of humanity the power of Christ shines with a Shekinah, but it is a glory more wonderful than that which overshadowed the ancient Tabernacle of Israel, and brings a transfiguring and healing virtue to those hearts in which it makes its home.

## CHAPTER XVIII

## THE THIRD HEAVEN

ST. PAUL speaks with a certain reserve of that wonderful trance in which he was caught up to Paradise and heard unspeakable words.[1] He penetrated to the 'third heaven' (*tritos ouranos*); and the mystic number, according to Calvin, signifies *par excellence* the highest and most perfect heaven. Yet he will not boast of this state to a people inclined perhaps to lay undue stress on visions and ecstatic utterances. He even describes the episode objectively, though this may be explained by the fact that he regards himself as another man, no longer what he was fourteen years before. No one, however, doubts that he is recounting a real and personal, albeit abnormal, experience. 'Whether in the body, I cannot tell; or whether out of the body, I cannot tell.' 'No words,' says Plumptre, 'can describe more accurately the phenomena of consciousness in the state of trance or ecstasy. The body remains sometimes standing, sometimes recumbent, but in either case motionless. The man may well doubt on his return to the normal condition of his life whether his spirit has actually passed into unknown regions in a separate and disembodied condition, or whether the body itself

[1] 2 Cor. xii. 1-5.

has been also a sharer in its experiences of the unseen.' The same writer refers to the fact that similar phenomena are recorded in the history of men like Pythagoras, Socrates, Plotinus, Mahomet, Francis of Assisi, Savonarola, George Fox, and Swedenborg.

The subject was invested many years ago with a vivid interest by a striking article in *The Spectator*,[1] entitled ' Vastness and Isolation,' in which there is a discussion of the meaning of the well-known lines in Wordsworth's *Ode on the Intimations of Immortality* :

> Those obstinate questionings
> Of sense and outward things:
> Fallings from us, vanishings,
> Blank misgivings of a creature
> Moving about in worlds not realized.

The writer concluded that the poet was alluding ' to a mental state in which isolation and vastness are the dominant characteristics. The material world, the whole universe indeed, seems to fall away from the person who experiences this mental condition, and he stands, as it were, a naked soul in a limitless cosmos, thrilled by the sense of immensity both as regards his own spirit and as regards the too vast orb of his fate.' He quoted also, in illustration of this mental condition, passages from Kinglake's *Eothen*, from the autobiographical experiences of J. A. Symonds and Berlioz the composer, and from other sources. There can be little doubt that he has given the right interpretation of Wordsworth's

[1] April 20, 1901. See also April 27 (' Correspondence ').

lines, though one may reasonably question whether the poet had any sense of terror or agony while in this extraordinary mood. Subsequently a correspondent in the same periodical offered striking corroboration of the view given of the above lines by relating how Professor Bonamy Price once asked the poet, in the course of a walk, what he meant by the words, ' Fallings from us,' &c. Wordsworth's answer was to this effect : ' Sometimes I find myself in a mood in which the whole material universe seems to fall away ; the sense of outward things is lost ; nothing remains but an immaterial self detached from all physical conditions. In order to get back into the known world of consciousness I have to clutch at something—so ' ; and here he grasped the bar of the gate on which they were leaning at the moment.[1]

This is certainly interesting, but it is doubtful whether the exact significance of such an experience, at least in Wordsworth's case, and possibly in that of others, is fully defined. Does the mood involve solely, or even chiefly, a sense of ' vastness and isolation ' ? Is it not rather in its essence, in its inwardness, a rapturous communion with the soul of all things ? The leading feature of such mystic ecstasy is not really isolation, but fellowship, or at least an isolation from the things of the material world which amounts to a joyous communion with

[1] See also Wordsworth's own note prefixed to the poem (Macmillan's edition of poems, p. 357).

the Unseen. It is not a Nirvana, an extinction of consciousness, or an absorption in the All-soul—ideas familiar to the student of Oriental religions; it is rather such an experience as we find described in Plato, from whom Wordsworth derives some of the philosophical ideas that pervade the great ode. For example, in the *Phaedo* Plato expounds the belief that true knowledge belongs to the soul alone. So long as the soul is bound up with the body, its passions, its weakness, and its pains, the soul is hampered and impaired in its apprehension of the truth. But when the partnership of body and soul is broken, then, but not till then, the soul realizes the joy of pure and untroubled contemplation. Immortality, therefore, is essential to the highest knowledge; in other words, the soul is set free not to an eternal isolation, but to a closer and more vivid affinity with the 'ideas'—those abiding, ultimate forms of which earthly things are but faint shadows or copies.[1] Undoubtedly Wordsworth, whether he consciously follows Plato or not, teaches that there are moments *even now* when the soul has these unclouded intuitions of the spiritual world—has 'sight of that immortal sea which brought us hither.' His conception of nature is dominated by the belief that it is alive—informed and interpenetrated by a living Spirit, an immanent Mind. Open

---

[1] In the same great work we find, too, the theory of 'recollection' as a proof of pre-existence, which we find embodied in Wordsworth's poem.

## The Third Heaven

Wordsworth anywhere, and the prevailing note is the harmony of all things—the 'ceaseless intercommunion' of every form of life. His idea of communion with nature is the fellow-feeling of the thinking soul of man with the Spirit of the universe; and there are times when the communion takes the form of joyous ecstasy. Take the famous passage in *The Excursion* describing the sensations of the youthful herdsman as he watches the sunrise:

> His spirit drank
> The spectacle: sensation, soul, and form
> All melted in him: they swallowed up
> His animal being; in them did he live,
> And by them did he live: they were his life.
>
> In such access of mind, in such high hour
> Of visitation from the living God,
> Thought was not: in enjoyment it expired.
> No thanks he breathed, he proffered no request;
> Rapt into still communion that transcends
> The imperfect offices of prayer and praise,
> His mind was a thanksgiving to the Power
> That made him: it was blessedness and love.

*The Excursion* is full of this note. Witness the rapture of the Solitary in a great storm among the lonely hills. Mists and vapours fleet past him like phantoms; streams dash down the mountain sides, and start up in the valleys; but there is no sense of isolation.

> What a joy to roam
> An equal among mightiest energies.

Wherever man moves in nature, he is in presence of the all-pervading Spirit:

> Spirit that knows no insulated spot,
> No chasm, no solitude.

Again, in a glowing passage on old age, which he describes as a final eminence, a throne of sovereignty and power, the poet conceives of the aged man removed from the stress of life not for utter loss, but to receive

> Fresh power to commune with the invisible world,
> And hear the mighty stream of tendency
> Uttering for elevation of our thought
> A clear sonorous voice, inaudible
> To the vast multitude; whose doom it is
> To run the giddy round of vain delight,
> Or fret and labour on the plain below.

It is needless to multiply quotations. According to Wordsworth, the soul surrenders itself to the Spirit that moves in all things, and becomes conscious that material things are slipping away; but in its detachment from the world of the senses it is thrilled with joy—the joy of a deeper fellowship with the Unseen—of entrance into the secret place of the Most High.

May not the Wordsworthian mood be only a modern parallel of St. Paul's experience of the third heaven? 'Of such an one,' says the Apostle, 'will I glory; yet of myself I will not glory but in my infirmities.' There is a wistful, pathetic cadence in these words. He looks back to those days of

## The Third Heaven

mystic contemplation when he received 'visions and revelations of the Lord.' His spirit was exuberant and buoyant at the beginning of his ministry. But the care of all the churches has told its tale. Infirmities have worn down his physical frame. In the anxieties of life, in the rush and movement of 'the good fight,' in the strain of the daily conflict, he walks by faith. His glorying now is not in mystic ecstasy, in supersensual moods, but in the marks of the Lord Jesus which he bears on his body. Does he ask, like the poet:

> Whither is fled the visionary gleam,
> Where is it now, the glory and the dream?

Here is the poet's self-consolation:

> We will grieve not, rather find
> Strength in what remains behind,
> In the primal sympathy
> Which having been must ever be;
> In the soothing thoughts that spring
> Out of human suffering,
> In the faith that looks through death,
> In years that bring the philosophic mind.

St. Paul's somewhat saddening retrospect is curiously paralleled not only by these words, but by the poet's explanatory statement prefixed to the ode: 'I was often unable to think of external things as having external existence, and I communed with all that I saw as something not apart from, but inherent in, my own immaterial nature. . . . At that time I was afraid of such processes. In later periods of life I have deplored, as we have all reason to do, a subjugation of an opposite character, and have rejoiced over the remembrances, as is expressed in the lines :

> Obstinate questionings
> Of sense and outward things,
> Fallings from us, vanishings, &c.'

'A subjugation of an opposite character.' The words are pathetic. Does our idealism fade with the years? Does the impact of material things deaden our souls? Are those visions and revelations, those upliftings to the third heaven in which we once rejoiced, now mere memories? It need not be so. The apocalypse of St. John was succeeded by the Gospel, the sudden ethereal vision by the abiding communion with the Eternal Word.[1] Faith in its maturity finds its joy not in the abnormal experiences of spiritual emotion and rapture, but in calm, serene converse with the Unseen. The saint whose soul has been chastened by the sufferings and changes of life may no longer be capable or conscious of celestial flights, of mounting up with wings as eagles into the very blaze and glory of the divine Presence; but he *walks* and does not faint. He moves daily in the heavenly places, and he knows that the goal of his journeying is an inheritance that fadeth not away. 'Eye hath not seen, nor ear heard, neither have entered the heart of man, the things which God hath prepared for them that love Him.'

---

[1] cf. John xxi. 22 : 'If I will that he *tarry* till I come, what is that to thee?'

## CHAPTER XIX

## HYPERBOLES OF FAITH

A DISTINCTIVE mark of St. Paul's style is his use of superlative terms and phrases such as verbs and adverbs compounded of *hyper*. In the majority of cases the prefix *hyper-* is an intensive form of the original local significance of the preposition = 'over,' 'beyond.' We may begin with the verb *hyperballo,* from which the word 'hyperbole' is derived. The Greek substantive, it may be noted, occurs chiefly in an adverbial phrase well rendered by the French *par excellence,* which is found five times in the Epistles and in 2 Cor. iv. 7, where we have the phrase intensified into a highly superlative expression translated by Moffatt, ' past all comparison ' ; but there are two interesting passages, 2 Cor. iv. 7, xii. 7, where *hyperbole* is found as a qualitative noun denoting excellence. Nothing can be inferred from the use of the verb, which, if a favourite with St. Paul, is yet the natural word to express the idea of pre-eminence or surpassingness, and is found as a participial epithet with '*greatness*' (Eph. i. 19), '*wealth*' (*ibid.* ii. 7), '*love*' (*ibid.* iii. 19), where it further qualifies the succeeding '*knowledge*,' and finally in 2 Cor. ix. 14 with '*grace*.'[1]

[1] There is an interesting use of '*hyperballo*' in *The Oxyrhynchus Papyri* (Grenfell & Hunt, 513, 25), where it is found in the passive, of a house for which a higher bid has been made.

We cannot consider his use of a whole set of adverbs and of verbs compounded with this preposition. It would be going too far to assert that this type of phraseology is peculiarly Pauline; for the Apostolic fathers give us examples of such verbs. It is possible, of course, that the sub-apostolic writers unconsciously or even deliberately copied a mark of style which was familiar to them from its prominence in the Pauline letters. But it is a more probable explanation that such exaggerated forms of expression are due to the more free and popular Greek in which Early Christian literature was written. We cannot regard even the least familiar of them as Pauline coinages with any certainty, though specific forms may with some confidence be described as hyperboles thrown off by St. Paul in a moment of ethical or spiritual emotion and therefore a speciality of his own. It is a somewhat subtle question how far popular style and the emotional mood or mentality of the individual writer affected the choice or creation of such hyperbolical expressions as have been cited above.

The dullness of this somewhat linguistic exordium will be relieved if we now look at a few of the more familiar examples of those *hyper*-verbs in St. Paul and attempt a brief exposition of them.

1. 'We are more than conquerors through Him that loved us' (Rom. viii. 37). Rendel Harris has translated the Greek in a manner which vividly represents the original (*hypernikōmen*) to the English reader by 'we *over*—overcome.' Moffatt retains the

beautiful 'we are more than conquerors' of the Geneva Version, found also in the A.V. and R.V. Tertullian and Cyprian (quoted by Sanday-Headlam, *in loc.*) translate the Greek by *supervincimus*—a coinage which certainly does more justice to St. Paul than the colourless *superamus* of the Vulgate. Tyndale's 'overcome strongly' is not as good as Coverdale's 'we conquer far.' The Christian life is a continuous victory—that is the first idea given by the word used in the present tense. The second idea is that it is not one of those victories which cost as much to the conqueror as to the conquered. There *is* a cost for victory to the Christian, whether the fight be against sin or sorrow or life's disabilities. Victory leaves its mark on the body: it sometimes produces the reaction of mental depression: it puts us out of harmony with our surroundings: it modifies—sometimes breaks the relationships of a lifetime, and its immediate result may be a sense of loneliness almost too bitter to be borne. Yet these are but the accidents of the experience of spiritual conquest. Within the soul itself there is a reinforcement of faith, hope, and love; the will has received an added force: to quote Rendel Harris (*Memoranda Sacra*, p. 184), we 'rise the stronger for the strife even while we strive.' Moffatt quotes, *in loc.* (*Literary Illustrations of the Bible*), the saying of Nelson on the Battle of the Nile, 'Victory is not a name strong enough for such a scene.' St. Paul likewise in effect says, 'Victory is not the name for the Christian's achievement': it is victory and something more: it is 'grace for grace': it is not merely a successful issue to which we 'muddle through' with much faltering and many errors; not a breathless impetus that just grips the point to be aimed at, like some rock-climber almost spent: it is an impetus that carries us beyond the issue, nerved and exhilarated, to meet the test that comes next. It is the love which Tennyson speaks of:

> that rose on stronger wings,
> Unpalsied when he met with Death.

2. 'The grace of our Lord abounded exceedingly (*hyperepleonasen*) (1 Tim. i. 14). Here the simple verb would suffice to express the abounding fulness of the stream of divine grace. 'The river of God is full of water,' says the Psalmist. To St. Paul the grace of Christ is a river 'in spate,' or an overflowing flood. Some such metaphor is necessary in rendering the word to which the A.V. 'was exceedingly abundant,' and the R.V. 'abounded exceedingly,' hardly do justice: hence the excellence of Moffatt's version, 'The grace of our Lord *flooded my life* along with the faith and love that Christ Jesus inspires.'

3. 'God hath highly exalted him' (*hyperypsōsen*) (Phil. ii. 9, A.V. and R.V.): 'God raised him high' (Moffatt). I venture to think that each of these renderings might convey the impression that a colourless word like the uncompounded verb was in the text. The statement is a climax of no ordinary force and splendour coming as it does after the

## Hyperboles of Faith

sublime passage—one of the greatest in all Christian literature and the source of theologies and homilies innumerable—in which St. Paul expounded the Incarnation, in its progress from an externally pre-existent life to a humiliation in time and a voluntary obedience to the extent of death upon a cross. The words compress in wonderful fashion the essence of the Christian creed and also its ethic. A translation of the actual expression adequate to its emotional intensity and majestic dignity is not easy; but I may quote the paraphrase which I had once the good fortune to hear from the lips of James Hope Moulton, 'Wherefore God made him the SUPERMAN.' The Nietzschean ideal of colossal soulless efficiency, the aristocracy of scientific Intellectuals dead to love, pity, and self-sacrifice, vanishes like a hideous nightmare before the radiant Redeemer, whom a great artist of the Spirit has depicted with immortal beauty and sureness of touch. The soul of man yearns for One 'mighty to save,' because pre-eminent in Love, regnant because crucified, Lord of humanity because obedient to death.

> My starry wings
> I do forsake,
> Love's highway of humility to take:
> Meekly I fit my stature to your need.
> In beggar's part
> About your gates I shall not cease to plead
> As man, to speak with man—
> Till by such art
> I shall achieve My Immemorial Plan,
> Pass the low lintel of the human heart.[1]

[1] E. Underhill, *Immanence*.

4. 'Your faith groweth exceedingly' (*hyperauxanei*) (2 Thess. i. 3, A.V. and R.V.); 'Your faith grows apace' (Moffatt). This great encourager of the saints does not use the simple 'groweth,' but characteristically intensifies the idea. He even goes beyond the 'aboundeth' which immediately succeeds and is connected with love (cf. another favourite word, '*abound* [*perisseuein*] more and more,' also united with the idea of Christian love in 1 Thess. iv. 10). It is the *faith* of his converts which he singles out for his special praise in this passage. It not only grows, but grows in exceptional measure or ratio. By the apostle, indeed, Love and Faith can never be regarded as other than superabundant; he thinks of both in terms of superfluity, and like high heaven

> rejects the lore
> Of nicely calculated less or more.

The Church has always had both, but has the Church ever yet risen to the height of the Pauline standard? Are we being lifted to it in despite of ourselves by the present crisis of our civilization? Love now as ever is called upon to quicken its pace and strain every effort in an awakened passion for the welfare and peace of mankind: it has to obey the call of duty and loyalty to the claims of the Spirit of God. But this implies a mighty faith. Is Faith equal to the tests of the age? It is Faith which operates through Love, as St. Paul asserts (Gal. v. 6). Faith must not waver. It must arise and laying aside all torpor and faint-heartedness 'mew its mighty youth.' Faith is essential to the triumph of Love. Once more, the Christian has to learn amid the anxieties and throes of a changing age to lean on a higher Power and to pray :

> O living will that shalt endure
>   When all that seems shall suffer shock,
>   Rise in the spiritual rock,
> Flow through our deeds and make them pure.

# GREEK WORDS

| | PAGE | | PAGE |
|---|---|---|---|
| ἀποκαραδοκία | 55 | καιρός | 41 |
| ἀφοράω | 55 | κοινωνία | 78 |
| αἴνιγμα | 125 | κτίσις | 56 |
| ἀκαιρῶς | 102 | μακροθυμία | 94 |
| αὐτάρκης | 118 | | |
| βαθμός | 27 | ὀσμή | 25 |
| βράβευς | 12 | παρρησία | 48 |
| βραβεύω | 12 | πλήρωμα | 110 |
| γνῶσις | 25 | πραιτώριον | 88 |
| εἰλικρίνεια | 63 | τέλειος | 79 |
| εἰρήνη | 11 | τρίτος οὐρανός | 141 |
| ἐξαγοράζομαι | 41 | ὑπεραυξάνω | 154 |
| ἐξῶθεν | 72 | ὑπερβάλλω | 149 |
| ἐπιείκεια | 33 | ὑπερβολή | 149 |
| ἐπισκηνόω | 135 | ὑπερνικάω | 150 |
| ἐπουράνιος | 110 | ὑπερπλεονάζω | 152 |
| ἔσοπτρον | 125 | ὑπομονή | 94 |
| εὐκαιρῶς | 102 | | |
| | | φρουρέω | 15 |
| θρίαμβος | 19 | | |
| θριαμβεύω | 19 | χρόνος | 42 |

www.ingramcontent.com/pod-product-compliance
Lightning Source LLC
Chambersburg PA
CBHW050824160426
43192CB00010B/1889